GATORS GLORY

Great Eras in Florida Football

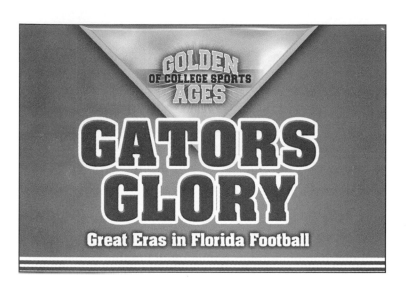

GOLDEN AGES
OF COLLEGE SPORTS

GATORS
GLORY

Great Eras in Florida Football

WILTON SHARPE

CUMBERLAND HOUSE
NASHVILLE, TENNESSEE

GATORS GLORY
PUBLISHED BY CUMBERLAND HOUSE PUBLISHING, INC.
431 Harding Industrial Drive
Nashville, TN 37211–3160

Cover design: Gore Studio, Inc.
Text design: John Mitchell
Research assistance/data entry: Caroline Ross

Content was compiled from a variety of sources and appears as originally presented; thus, some factual errors and differences in accounts may exist.

Library of Congress Cataloging-in-Publication Data

Sharpe, Wilton.
  Gators glory : great eras in Florida football / Wilton Sharpe.
    p. cm.
  Includes bibliographical references and index.
  ISBN-13: 978-1-58182-621-0 (pbk. : alk. paper)
  ISBN-10: 1-58182-621-4 (pbk. : alk. paper)
  1. University of Florida—Football—History. 2. Florida Gators (Football team)—History. I. Title.

  GV958.U523S53 2007
  796.332'630975979—dc22
  [B]
                                                              2007023861

Printed in the United States of America

1 2 3 4 5 6 7—13 12 11 10 09 08 07

For Caroline,
and many more happy years together

CONTENTS

FOREWORD

As a skinny Connecticut-bred boy, my first exposure to Florida football was through a diminutive quarterback of the early 1960s named Larry Libertore, a skittery little water bug-like creature who always seemed to connect on the important pass. I quarterbacked my high school football team the same years that Libertore was delighting the Florida faithful with his squirmy antics in the open field. My efforts, in comparison, fell woefully short of matching the wizard-like results that Little Larry regularly produced.

Not long after came the Spurrier years (as a player), and the Gators were on their way. Though the timeline of Florida football did not begin to turn to a golden hue until the 1990s, there is a rich undertone to the many decades leading up to the Spurrier-as-coach era and, currently, the Urban Meyer reign. To be certain, Gator fans have experienced their share of frustration, perhaps longer than any other major university in America. But few would doubt that they're making up for lost time now: two national championships in the last decade and seven SEC championships in the last 16 years.

Gators Glory takes you from early greats Cannonball Crabtree and Carl Brumbaugh to Haywood Sullivan and Rick Casares through the Steve Spurrier era to the Reaves-Alvarez years; from Nat Moore, Wes Chandler, Wilber Marshall, Alonzo Johnson and beyond to Emmitt, Errict, Reidel, Danny, Chris, Tim, Percy, and all the Gator greats who have contributed (and are still adding) to the dynamic UF legacy.

Gators Glory is in effect a collective autobiography of University of Florida football, whose authors are the voices of UF players, coaches, opposing players and coaches, media, and fans—all recounting the Gators' major moments, legends, legendary coaches, great quarterbacks, outstanding teams, and great rivalries. It is an endless source of recollection on Florida's illustrious gridiron past.

From Rhett to Rex, Weary to Wuerffel, Marshall to Matthews, Little Larry to Leak, and Tannen to Tebow . . . it's all Gators!

— W.S.

ORIGINS

I must say, I thought after that 144–0 game that college football was a piece of cake. Auburn instructed me otherwise.

Rex Farrior

(1913–16),
on the Gators' humbling 55–0 loss to the
Plainsmen in 1913, the week following their
record win over Florida Southern

In the beginning, there were . . . two?

University of Florida football actually has two beginnings.

Two schools, Florida Agricultural College and East Florida Seminary, which began as early as the 1860s, were merged by the Buckman Bill in 1905 into the present-day University of Florida, with a student body first appearing in 1906.

Our story begins with the gridiron efforts undertaken at Florida Agricultural College, in Lake City, in 1899—seven years before the University of Florida's football records begin.

During this pre-UF period, FAC began playing a school in Tallahassee called Florida State College, from 1902–1904. In the same legislative action that united FAC and EFS into UF in 1905, Florida State College became Florida State College for Women. Football fans yearning for head-to-head competition between Florida and what would later become known as Florida State University would have to wait 53 more years for the two natural rivals to meet again.

In the meantime, the embryonic efforts of FAC, followed by the University of Florida, began to unfold. Beginnings were humble for the most part, but ultimately UF's tribulations gave way to an indomitable "Fighting Gators" spirit.

T he football player of today is so well protected by modern rules of the game, as well as by his equipment, that his chances of being hurt are no greater than those of the average bicycle or horseback rider. This season, our Commandant took charge of the training of the squad and personally conducted their exercises to guarantee that the work was done thoroughly. To show that the training was not done with intent to kill anybody, let us add that we were very materially aided by the advice and coaching of professors Blair (A. W., chemistry) and Miller (H. K., chemistry), and of a minister of the Gospel, the Reverend Mr. Tims, of the Presbyterian Church.

1899–1900 Florida Agricultural College Yearbook

(predecessor of the University of Florida)

The team entertained very strong hopes of meeting some other teams during the past season, but owing to circumstances over which we had no control we were unable to get the games we so desired, but we have hopes for the future.

1899–1900 Florida Agricultural College Yearbook

FAC, though it fielded a team, played no one its first year

Acquisition of uniforms and equipment was up to the team. Each player scrounged for his own quilted pants, jersey, and football shoes. Somehow the team was organized and practiced, and arrangements were made for the first game.

Tom McEwen

former Tampa Tribune/Tampa Times *sports editor/author, on FAC's fledgling football efforts*

It is the first battle in the royal game, the game that calls out the best resources, the pluck, the endurance, and speed of lusty young manhood between these two great colleges.

Florida Times-Union

*November 22, 1901,
heralding the Florida Agricultural College-
Stetson tilt, the future University
of Florida's first-ever game of
collegiate football*

The ball is now only eight yards from Stetson's goal line. A stump in the field interfered with the play and the ball had to be carried to one side, to Lake City's disadvantage. That stopped the drive.

Florida Times-Union

*November 23, 1901,
Stetson defeated FAC, 6–0*

L ast Friday, the people of Lake City witnessed a game of football between the teams of Florida Agricultural College and Florida State College of Tallahassee. Although the game was hotly contested from the first, it was plain the local team was the stronger, and the ball moved steadily through Tallahassee's field. A touchdown was made by a 20-yard run by C. H. Maguire and a 10-yard run by McCaskell. The first half ended in a score of 6 to 0 in favor of the local team (FAC). No points were scored by either in the second half.

Lake City Reporter

1902,
on the first "UF-FSU" game—
won by FAC, the future Florida Gators. FSU
was called the Florida State College
of Tallahassee

I t must have been particularly embarrassing even then for Florida to lose to a team from Tallahassee because after the loss the coach, Fleming, quit and "returned to Jackson to resume his law practice," an account reported.

Tom McEwen

on the 12–0 loss to Florida State College in 1903

S tetson was the big rivalry. Those fellows had good teams. In 1903, I remember playing against a big fellow named Pounds. When the game began, with Pounds opposite me, I suggested that if he would not slug me, I would not slug him.

William Morrow Rowlett Jr.

former FAC lineman, at 91

O ur equipment was sparse. We wore those clumsy nose guards that came down across your cheeks and you held them between your teeth. Quite uncomfortable. And the rules were a bit sketchy. . . . At Alabama, when the going got tough, we resorted to grabbing each other by the belt to prevent the runner from coming between us.

William Morrow Rowlett Jr.

T he people of Gainesville are dedicated to football. Since the university has been established here and there is a good team with prospects of witnessing some fine games, interest increases.

The Gainesville Sun
1906,
after Florida Agricultural College merged with East Florida Seminary to form the University of Florida. Gainesville was chosen as the site of the institution

Football was so new at Florida in 1906–07 it still lacked a nickname. At times the team was referred to in print merely as "Pee Wee's Boys" for player-coach Pee Wee Forsythe.

Tom McEwen

I had no idea it would stick.

Austin Miller

*on the nickname "Alligators,"
which Miller suggested to his father and the
Michie Company—a manufacturer of school
pennants—sometime in the year 1908.
Austin's father, Philip, had placed an order for
some Florida pennants for his sundries shop,
and the transaction called for placing a
nickname after the school name*

I remember Rammy Ramsdell (1913–15) quarterbacking his first time, against The Citadel. He called for me to go off tackle. He called it again and again and again, until we'd marched the length of the field. I asked him why he'd not called any other plays, and urged that he do so. But he said he couldn't think of any of the others.

Jim Sparkman
halfback (1914–16, Captain '19)

All we gave by way of scholarships in those days were meals at Ma Rainey's and room to the top players who could not afford it.

Charley Bachman
head coach (1928–32)

GATOR TRADITION

He's been doing it for more than 50 years and very little of his brief but unforgettable routine has changed over the years. George Edmondson is Mr. Two Bits. And the tradition he started on September 24, 1949, at the season opener between The Citadel and Florida is without a doubt the single most enduring tradition in the century-old history of Gator football.

David Stirt
author/editor

When you look around the walls in the south end zone and see all the great players and past Gator teams. You understand what a privilege it is to wear a Florida uniform. There have been so many amazing athletes in Gator history who will be remembered for years to come. Their success drives you to achieve at the highest levels.

Danny Wuerffel
quarterback (1993–96)

Coming out of the tunnel for an SEC game is a very special feeling. You can feel the passion and enthusiasm for college football. You can feel all of the history and tradition that has made the SEC the nation's premier football conference.

Errict Rhett
running back (1990–93)

Pre-Steve

The winning tradition at Florida, in most people's minds, tends to begin with two elements: the 1990s and Steve Spurrier. But though there were no Southeastern Conference championships, let alone a national title, before the Spurrier era began, that's not to say there wasn't success in Gainesville.

For instance, in Florida's first 25 years, there were only four losing campaigns. Admittedly the Depression-era '30s and post-World War II days of the mid- to late 1940s, during which UF posted just four winning seasons in 19 years, were dark days for Gator fans. But matters brightened considerably during the entire Ray Graves era of the 1960s, which yielded a total won-lost mark of 70–31–4 and included five bowl appearances, in which the Gators rang up a 4–1 record that encompassed the 27–12 Orange Bowl victory over Georgia Tech in 1967.

The mid-1970s and early to mid-1980s also produced exceptional Gator teams with glowing season records.

One of the many reasons why I, and so many others, came to Florida is because of the tradition. When you see the list of players that have played here, it truly becomes an honor to play on the same field as they have. . . . What's really exciting is the fact that everybody believes the best is yet to come.

Larry Kennedy
defensive back (1991–94)

The Florida defense is for winners. The players here are expected to go through hard-nose preparation and each member of the team expects the best effort from his teammates in order to keep this tradition strong.

Carlton Miles
inside linebacker (1989–92)

There is something about Florida that generates an incredible amount of attention and recognition as evidenced by the fact that 11 players earned All-America honors in 1991. Think about that. One-half of Florida's starters earned All-America honors. It is awesome, simply out of this world. As a team and individual, having Florida football as a part of your life means you will receive incredible recognition for what you and the team accomplish.

Hesham Ismail
guard (1988–91)

We've got a winning habit and tradition in the '90s at Florida, and certainly we've got a chance to continue being good. We're trying to be the best program in the state.

Steve Spurrier
quarterback (1964–66)/
assistant coach (1978)/
head coach (1990–2001)

ore than anyone, Steve Spurrier has been responsible for mending UF's broken home and for making Gators proud to be Gators again. Yeah, it's kind of corny the way Spurrier gets misty-eyed when he sings "We Are the Boys" or the way he makes his players stay out on Florida Field after home games and sing the alma mater, but there is no doubt he is genuine about making the Gator family whole again.

Mike Bianchi
Orlando Sentinel

Playing outside linebacker at Florida is both a great honor and a tremendous challenge. It is part of a tradition that is larger than any one or two people.

Ty Smith
assistant coach (1983–87)

I have followed college football very closely for 30 or 40 years and I really believe the University of Florida, in the past five or six years, has written a whole new chapter in college football.

Bill Clinton
42nd president of the United States, 1997

T he tradition of playing "We Are The Boys" at the end of the third quarter is so popular that during a game in 2003, after fans had finished singing and swaying, officials decided time had not run out in the period and put several seconds back on the clock for one more third-quarter play. After the play was over, the band struck up "We Are the Boys" a second time and the fans were delighted to repeat their part of the popular ritual.

David Stirt

THE BLUE
& ORANGE

*W*hen the roll of great football players at the University of Florida is called, familiar names immediately surface: Spurrier, Wuerffel, Marshall, Kearse, Hilliard, Emmitt Smith, Chris Leak, and the like. But the awe of an Emmitt, the joy of a Jevon, or the wonder of a Wuerffel are all the more valued when placed against the backdrop of players less known, but who performed with no less fervor, excellence, and commitment: The Dummy Taylors, Ark Newtons, Jimmy Dunns, Larry Rentzes, Chris Doerings, and Willie Jackson Jrs.

Herein lies a sampling of Gators who have paved the path of Florida football through the 20th century and beyond.

Dummy Taylor has stood out as a pre-eminent star like none heretofore. To Dummy (real name, Earle) must go the credit more than any other man of putting Florida on the football map, and it is with regret we realize that his football days are a thing of the past.

The Alligator
December 17, 1912

> **FAST FACT:** *QB-HB Taylor played for the Gators in 1908 and from 1910 through 1912.*

I'd have to judge Ark Newton my best. He had an unorthodox style and we tried to change it. That was a mistake. He went back to his own style and was often a savior to us.

Major James A. Van Fleet
head coach (1923–24)

He was a superb punter and a classic broken field runner, fearless and football-wise.

Tom McEwen
on Ark Newton (1921–24)

Walter Mayberry is as good a back as I ever saw. He was smart and he could pass and kick.

D. K. Stanley
head coach (1933–35)

Both Mayberry and Fergie Ferguson rank on all-time Florida teams, and observers of Florida football over the years agree that they would be heroes today.

Tom McEwen

Buford Long could run. You get him outside, get him loose, and he was pretty tough to catch.

Haywood Sullivan

quarterback (1950–51),
on the Gators' halfback of 1950–52.
Long went on to play three seasons with the
New York Giants

Vel Heckman's play, superb all season, reached All-America level against LSU and Auburn. Big, fast, and tough, he outshone all of Auburn's great linemen.

Bill Kastelz

former Jacksonville Times-Union
sports editor,
on Florida's 1958 All-America tackle

Bruce Bennett, a little guy from Orlando, was voted on the All-Century team as the best defensive back in the history of Florida.

Richard Trapp

flankerback (1965–67),
on the Gator DB from 1963 through '65

T here is no one receiver in the South any better than Richard Trapp.

Bobby Dodd
legendary Georgia Tech head coach

I 'm not sure, but I think it was five.

Richard Trapp
asked how many tacklers had a shot at him on his electrifying 52-yard touchdown pass reception against Georgia in the Gators' 17–16 win over the Bulldogs in 1967. On the play, Trapp took a 12-yard pass from quarterback Larry Rentz, reversed his direction, dodged a pair of defenders, cut up toward the right sideline, and escaped at least three more Bulldog tacklers before reaching the end zone

I 've said it before that Richard Trapp is the most dangerous man, once he catches the ball, that I've seen as a receiver.

Ray Graves
head coach (1960–69)

R ichard Trapp is just a great athlete. I don't think there's anything he can't do. He was billiards champion of the University of Florida. He won the over-40 national ping-pong championships. A few years ago he won a tennis championship. He played professional baseball and football. I don't know any sport he's not accomplished in.

Larry Smith
running back (1966–68)

R ichard Trapp was so good. I would throw a pass that was off, but he would catch it. He made a quarterback look good.

Larry Rentz
defensive back/quarterback (1966–68)

Larry Rentz was a great athlete, like Richard Trapp. There was nothing Larry couldn't do, whether it was golf or baseball or tennis or football. He was a tough player and very quick. We used to tease him about being able to dodge raindrops.

Larry Smith

Jimmy Fisher was a great athlete, one of the smartest, brightest, friendliest guys. He always had a smile on his face. He never said a negative word about anybody. Jimmy was a heady guy who meant a lot to the program at the time. He was just a good athlete who never got the chance to play at the next level.

Scot Brantley
*linebacker (1976–79),
on the Gators' mid-'70s quarterback*

My tight end was Jimmy Ray Stephens. I still think Jimmy is the greatest athlete ever at the University of Florida. He started at three positions in three years.

Jimmy Fisher
quarterback (1974–76)

He was a gutsy fighter of a guy. He was small, didn't have that great an arm, but was just a fighter.

Wayne Peace
quarterback (1980–83)
on quarterback Larry Ochab (1979–80)

Bob Hewko was not a physical guy but was a heck of a quarterback. He made good decisions and made the best of his abilities. You have to give him a lot of credit, because the year before, the 1979 team had been 0–10–1, and he just came in and played extremely well.

Wayne Peace

Neal Anderson starred as a running back for the Gators (1982–1985) and led them in rushing for three seasons (1983–1985). He became only the second Gator to rush for more than 1,000 yards (1,034 in 1985) and is now third on the career yardage list with 3,234 yards, behind Errict Rhett and Emmitt Smith.

Kevin M. McCarthy
author

Ricky Nattiel is an exciting player, a game-breaker with great speed. If everybody else plays to a Mexican stand-off he can win the game for you.

Galen Hall
offensive coordinator (1984)/
head coach (1984–89),
on the UF wide receiver from 1983
through '86

Offensive tackle David Williams, who lettered for four years (1985–1988) and was named to UF's Team of the Century in 1999, started in every game in his UF career (46), after which he played in the NFL for the Houston Oilers (1989–1995) and New York Jets (1996–1997).

Kevin M. McCarthy

Harrison Houston was only about 5'8", but he was extremely fast. He didn't have the greatest hands—he couldn't catch anything in practice. He dropped balls left and right. But when the game started, he was one of the most reliable receivers I had.

Shane Matthews
quarterback (1990–92)/
1990 and '91 SEC Player of the Year,
on the Gators wideout from 1990 through '93

Willie Jackson Jr. was probably the most talented receiver I ever played with at Florida. He was about 6'3", 215 pounds, not as fast as most people want their receivers to be, but he was the kind of guy who made plays after the ball was in his hands. Whenever I needed someone to come up with a big play, Willie was the guy I always looked for. He was the kind of receiver Coach Spurrier liked, big and strong. He was a freshman walk-on who came out of nowhere. He's the son of Willie Jackson, who was the first black to play at the university.

Shane Matthews

Shane Edge (1991–94) could boom that ball. He was a great athlete who could dunk a basketball. . . . In order to do great things in life, you've got to stick your neck out a little bit. Edge was that type of kid. He took the risk.

Paul Bowen
wide receiver (1994)

Shane Edge was not your typical punter. He could two-hand slam a basketball. He could do a 360 slam. He was a pretty spectacular athlete.

Terry Dean
quarterback (1991–94)

hris Doering (1993–95) is a great story. He was a walk-on who earned a chance to play. He wasn't the fastest or the strongest, but he had the most heart—a real tall guy who ran real precise routes. He appreciated being out on the field every minute. Most guys don't appreciate it until after it's over. Chris never took anything for granted. He was living his dream, and it showed.

Danny Wuerffel

hen Reidel Anthony got the ball, he could really make things happen. It's what made our offense go. We had four or five guys, when they touched the ball, they could score from anywhere on the field.

Terry Jackson
running back (1995–98)

R eidel Anthony was a great player. He was more of a Jerry Rice type of receiver. He was tall and smooth, wasn't real physical, more of a glider. He ran precise routes, and he had great speed.

Danny Wuerffel

R eidel Anthony's got Ernie Mills's speed, Willie Jackson's tenacity to go after the ball, Harrison Houston's quickness to make people miss, and he makes the big catches like Chris Doering.

Dwayne Dixon
receivers coach (1990–2004)

I feel like I'm unstoppable. That's not arrogance, that's just part of being confident.

Reidel Anthony
wide receiver (1994–96)

Derrick Harvey is the most under-rated player in the nation. He came out of nowhere this year. People need to recognize what he has done.

Steven Harris
*defensive tackle (2003–06),
on the 2006 BCS National Championship
Game Defensive MVP. Harvey, a 6-foot-5,
262-pounder, registered three sacks,
four tackles, and a recovered fumble
in the Gators' 41–14 rout of No. 1 Ohio State.
On the season, Harvey recorded 11 sacks
and 35 tackles*

P ercy Harvin changed the game on offense. Every time we're in a rut, that kid's a dynamic football player. We've got to give him the ball more.

Urban Meyer

*head coach (2005–),
on the Gators' game-breaking freshman wide
receiver/running back, following an explosive
performance in Florida's 17–16 victory over
South Carolina, on November 11, 2006, in
which Harvin pulled in six catches for 91
yards—including a crucial 19-yard reception
on UF's final scoring drive—and four rushes
for 20 more yards*

GATOR GRIT

ootball is a great team sport. It teaches you to respect other people. You can line the town drunk's son up by the doctor's son—it makes no difference out there, one of the few places where it's that way.

Larry Dupree
halfback (1962–64)

Coach Dickey looks you in the eye and tells you how it is, and that's what my dad taught me to do.

Carlos Alvarez
wide receiver (1969–71)

I'm a leader. If I kept moping and pouting, the young players would have given up, too. I had to accept the responsibility.

Fred Taylor
*running back (1994–97),
whose two early fumbles handed Florida
State 10 quick points in the 1997 intrastate
clash ultimately won by Florida 32–29. Taylor
later redeemed himself, scoring the winning
touchdown—his fourth of the afternoon—
while also grinding out 162 yards rushing*

I always try to improve.

Emmitt Smith
running back (1987–89)

We have a commitment to the concept of developing the total person as an individual, and not just as an athlete.

Galen Hall

This means that my hypocrisy has ceased.

Emmitt Smith

May 5, 1996,
upon receiving his degree from the
University of Florida six years after leaving
school to enter the NFL. Smith's "hypocrisy"
refers to his frequent speeches to youth
groups. His message? Stay in school and stay
off drugs

I think former players should know that, no matter what, they always have a home here. It's nice to belong to a group, a family, a team, and that doesn't have to end when you quit playing here.

Steve Spurrier

You want to either play for real or not play at all.

Kevin Carter
defensive end (1991–94)

You can recognize talent. But it's a bit harder to recognize mental toughness.

Fernando Storch
UF booster

Football is very important to those who are playing the game, but it is not the ultimate thing in your life. You need to keep in perspective the fact it is not a life-and-death matter or World War III. There must be self-sacrifice and discipline in order to achieve athletic success, but there must also be fun in playing the sport.

Galen Hall

If you're nasty, they're going to respect you. My motor was always running. If you keep your motor running, you don't have to take all those cheap shots because nobody can ever hit you. You're either down or you're up. But if you stand around you're going to get blasted.

Wilber Marshall
outside linebacker (1980–83)

He's got a gift. Not only athletically, but Wilber Marshall is a sensitive, deep person. . . . Wilber was one of the few people I'd trust with my son. I would've left Carrick with him for a month if necessary. That's how much I trusted him.

Charley Pell
head coach (1979–84)

If you want to get through a hole bad enough, you'll get through it.

Emmitt Smith

Emmitt is quiet, but he's so competitive. He wasn't a trash talker, but in my eyes the competitive fire in him was rivaled only by Walter Payton. Same type of guy. Maybe they didn't look the prettiest or were the biggest or strongest guy, but they win because they compete, they fight, and they scrap for everything they get. What Emmitt's done is a testimony to that kind of fire.

Jerry Odom
linebacker (1987–90)

Thinking about the Heisman is something that's completely out of our frame. It's something that's added on at the end of the season. Personal goals are things that are nice to have, but they are things that come later.

Danny Wuerffel

I saw it before the game. You look in guys' eyes; I liked what I saw.

Urban Meyer
on the Gators 21–20 come-from-behind victory over Tennessee in Knoxville in 2006

He's out there firing off the Gator chomp at 107,000 people. That's when I said, "You're returning kicks tonight."

Urban Meyer
on 2006 freshman running back Brandon James's pregame display in Knoxville. James returned four punts for 65 yards in the 21–20 victory over Tennessee

In football, you can get on that field and become just about what you want to become. You can be a monster in disguise. But if you're ever going to do well, you have to put heart and soul in it.

Larry Dupree

When you work hard, when you keep doing the right things and you are a good person, you get your schoolwork done, you graduate. When you are doing all the right things, eventually your time is going to come.

Chris Leak
quarterback (2003–06)/BCS 2006 National Championship Game MVP

GATOR
HUMOR

I t could be worse. We could have sched-
uled 10 games.

Ray "Bear" Wolf
head coach (1946–49)

FAST FACT: *Wolf's reign is incongruously known as the Golden Era of Florida Football. A tongue-in-cheek reference to the Gators' 13–39 record over Wolf's four years at the UF helm. His above quote speaks directly to Florida's pitiable 0–9 worksheet in 1946.*

S teve Spurrier's daddy is a preacher up in Tennessee, and "dadgum it" is about as tough as he's ever going to get. Once in a while, he'll get a little stronger when he gets completely frustrated.

Keith Jackson
longtime legendary college football announcer

I know you don't like being named Mr. Pancake. And as many times as people have mispronounced my name, maybe we should go into waffles.

Danny Wuerffel
to Orlando Pace, renowned for his pancake blocks on defensive linemen while at Ohio State, during Wuerffel's acceptance speech at the Heisman Trophy award ceremonies in New York in 1996

I'm telling you, if he'd have come down our sideline, 10 guys would've tackled him off the bench. He just ran down the wrong sideline.

Cris Collinsworth

on Georgia receiver Lindsay Scott's legendary game-winning catch against Florida in the heartbreaking, last-minute 26–21 loss to the Bulldogs in 1980

Now we know why buckeye trees don't grow in the desert. A Gator probably would come along and eat them.

David Whitley

*Orlando Sentinel writer,
following Florida's upset win over
No. 1-ranked Ohio State in the 2006 BCS
National Championship Game*

Among the traditions was the passing up of students, a popular exercise that took place several times a game when students in the lower east stands would pass a student up through the crowd until he or she was several dozen rows higher in the stands than they started. UF officials brought the tradition to a halt after some creative students dressed up a mannequin as a cheerleader, passed it all the way to the top of the east stands, before students on the top row threw the mannequin over the wall and out of the stadium to the horror of the alumni-packed west stands.

David Stirt

I knew Dr. Cade, the inventor of Gatorade. He also was the inventor of the helmet with water in it, but it was too heavy in its concept. He used my wife-to-be, who was a student at Florida then, as a model for that helmet. He put it on her and hit her over the head with a baseball bat. That's why she married me—she got hit over the head with a bat.

John Reaves
quarterback (1969–71)

A long time before they won anything, Gator fans had the arrogance of Alabama and the tradition of Wake Forest.

Dan Jenkins
novelist and noted sportswriter

I'll never forget watching him slow dance with my mom or doing the Macarena with my sister. After witnessing the Macarena episode, let me just say this about Coach Spurrier as a dancer: He's a tremendous play-caller.

Danny Wuerffel
following a small banquet in New York City feting previous Heisman Trophy winners

The Ohio State band did its traditional "dotting of the I" at halftime, but it was the Florida football team that did its nontraditional "crushing of the Buckeye" throughout the rest of the game.

Mike Bianchi
on the Gators' 2006 national championship game win over Ohio State

THE GREAT FLORIDA QUARTERBACKS

H e was the only quarterback I coached who I gave free hand to call a check-off on any play we called from the sideline. If you have a quarterback who can do that, you give him free reign, because the players on the field have more of a feeling for the game than you do on the sideline. He was just a player who would even check off after the ball was snapped, just by hand signals.

Ray Graves
on Steve Spurrier

About the most frustrating thing he'd do to the opposition was on third down he'd run to his right or left towards the sidelines, and if the safety came up (Clyde) Crabtree would punt over his head on the run, side-footed. What a weapon he was. He was a double-quadruple option. He could sprint out and had the option of running, passing (with either hand), handing off, or punting (with either foot). He was also a good receiver.

Charley Bachman
*on the ambidextrous, multi-talented
Clyde "Cannonball" Crabtree*

I learned to pass and kick on the run going either way from sheer fright. I weighed 110 pounds when I played high school ball.

Clyde Crabtree
quarterback (1927–29)

Clyde Crabtree was a Daniel Boone player: He played by instinct. That's not all. He had rubberband legs. He'd bounce around. He was never on the bottom of the pile.

Nash Higgins
assistant coach (1928–30)

A crop of fine sophomores made the outlook brighter. Included among them was a super quarterbacking prospect named Haywood Sullivan, the best-looking passer who had ever been in a Gator uniform.

Tom McEwen

FAST FACT: as a soph sensation in 1950, Sullivan became the first QB in SEC history to pass for over 1,000 yards in a season. But the brilliant Sullivan would only quarterback the Gators for two years, opting for a lucrative $75,000 "bonus baby" contract with the Boston Red Sox before his senior season.

Tall and lanky and the possessor of a golden throwing arm, Haywood Sullivan came to the University of Florida to escape having to choose between state rivals Alabama and Auburn.

Peter Golenbock
author

Haywood Sullivan

The game I remember most was our final game. It was Alabama's Homecoming, and they were heavy favorites. All the people from Dothan (Sullivan's hometown) who had been at the Auburn game, who had been disappointed by our 14–13 loss there, all seemed to gather for this game in Tuscaloosa. We had a great day. It was the highlight of all the games we ever played.

Haywood Sullivan
*on Florida's 30–21 win over the Tide
to climax the 1951 season*

We would have won the National Championship in '52 if Haywood Sullivan had stayed, because he was a great, great quarterback, and the rest of us were average. Still, no one held it against Haywood.

Bobby Lance
quarterback (1954–55)

I often hear the comment, "Where could we have gone? What bowl could you have gone to?" And you never know those things. I could have gotten hurt in the first game, or we could have had a lousy year and I would have gone on to the army and gotten killed. Who knows?

Haywood Sullivan
*on his unfulfilled senior year at UF.
Sullivan could not refuse the Boston
Red Sox's bonus offer of $75,000, and the
"what ifs" of 1952 became the topic of
endless debate*

ll Doug Dickey could do was win.

Bob Woodruff
*head coach (1950–59),
on quarterback [and future Florida head
coach] Dickey, who led the 1952 Gators to a
7–3 record and UF's first bowl game,
a 14–13 Gator Bowl victory over Tulsa*

J immy Dunn is pound for pound the best football player I ever coached.

Bob Woodruff

*on the diminutive 147-pound Gator QB
from 1956 through '58*

O ur quarterback in 1960 was Larry Libertore. He was as quick as a cat. If somebody didn't tackle him, he was gonna go. He was one of those jitterbugs with the big heart, like Jimmy Dunn. Same size—about 145 pounds, a fiery kind of guy, liked to have a lot of fun. He could turn a missed tackle into a 60-yard run.

Don Deal

halfback (1958–60)

The Gators had a little quarterback named Larry Libertore, so small that he shouldn't have been out without his governess.

Furman Bisher
Atlanta Journal, 1960

Steve Spurrier was someone everyone looked up to. You just had a lot of confidence in him. You thought you were going to win any game that you had a shot at winning as long as he was in there.

Richard Trapp

S teve Spurrier directed an attack that resulted in nine second-half comeback wins, eight of them in the fourth quarter. His skill and confidence under pressure astounded opponents, fans, and the media.

Norm Carlson

*longtime Gator sports information director/
assistant athletic director*

FAST FACT: *Carlson was the primary force behind Spurrier's Heisman Trophy publicity effort in 1966.*

H e was a real team guy. All the guys who played with him still root for him. Yeah, he was the leader. I don't know of anyone who didn't respect him or like him. So when he won [the Heisman Trophy], we were elated. Everybody was elated.

Larry Smith

on Steve Spurrier

I t took Steve Spurrier one series of plays to generate explosive excitement for the first time in his Florida Field career, two games to introduce his fourth-quarter heroics, three games to throw the bomb, and a half-season to verify that he was likely to be somebody real special before he ended his Southeastern Conference career....Merely the greatest quarterback in SEC history.

Joe Halberstein
The Gainesville Sun, *December 3, 1966*

S teve Spurrier is a real-life Frank Merriwell.

Joe Durso
The New York Times,
*on the playing career of 1966
Heisman Trophy winner Steve Spurrier*

UNIVERSITY OF FLORIDA

Steve Spurrier

In 1966, Gator fans referred to Spurrier as S.O.S.—not so much for his initials (Stephen Orr Spurrier) but for his propensity to come to the rescue and pull out victories in the fourth quarter.

Robbie Andreu

The Gainesville Sun

The week after the crushing 27–10 loss to Georgia, in which Spurrier was beaten up by the Bulldogs, the mood was somber at Florida Field. I remember watching Spurrier warm up before the game through my binoculars. He was so fluid, so effortless, so confident throwing the ball that he appeared to be moving in slow motion. The loss to Georgia hadn't changed him. He was still every bit a Florida hero.

Noel Nash

*editor,
on UF's 31–10 win over Tulane,
November 12, 1966*

He is the greatest quarterback ever in college football. He's like another coach; in fact, he's smarter than a lot of coaches.

Bill Peterson
*former head coach of Florida State,
on Steve Spurrier, after Peterson's Seminoles
lost to Spurrier and the Gators, 22–19,
in 1966*

Steve Spurrier is a great football player. He just picks your defense apart. He's poised, confident, smart. He knows what to do all the time. He's great on everything. It's hard to figure out how to defense him. I'll say it again, Steve Spurrier is a great one.

Bill Oliver
former Auburn defensive coordinator

By the half, they were comparing him to Florida's 1966 Heisman Trophy winner Steve Spurrier. By the end they asking, "Steve Who?"

Bill Clark
Orlando Sentinel, September 21, 1969, on the sizzling debut of sophomore QB John Reaves, who set three school passing records and tied one SEC mark in UF's season-opening rout of preseason (Playboy) No. 1 pick Houston, 59–34. Reaves's 70-yard scoring pass to wide receiver and fellow soph Carlos Alvarez occurred just one minute and 15 seconds into their college careers

You could see the talent in John Reaves. He was 6'4", 200 pounds, and he had that natural air of a quarterback. He could throw the football a country mile.

Jack Youngblood
defensive end (1968–70)

John Reaves is a good one, has everything it takes to be a great quarterback. He's cocky and always has been. I've known him from Tampa days way back and he was always that way. He ranks with the best, sure, right up there with Archic Manning or anybody you want to name.

Steve Kiner

Tennessee All-America linebacker, after the 1969 Gator Bowl loss to Florida

Don Gaffney was first class all the way. And he was a great competitor. He did not like getting beat.

Jimmy Dunn

quarterback (1956–58) / assistant coach (1960–63) / offensive coordinator (1970–77), on UF's first African-American quarterback

Don Gaffney played for three years (1973–1975). In '73 he was the starting quarterback of the first Gator team to win a game at Cliff Hare Stadium in Auburn. The Gators also defeated Georgia, FSU, and Miami all in the same month, a very rare feat.

Kevin M. McCarthy

Wayne Peace was a true freshman, a high school All-America, very highly recruited. When he got to campus, you could see he wasn't your regular everyday freshman. He was a big, strong kid, and he came in with a confidence about him. [Offensive coordinator] Mike Shanahan had a great offense, and Wayne was able to pick it up real quick. He knew where and when to throw the ball.

Tim Groves
quarterback (1978–80)

K erwin Bell is an inspiring story. He goes to Florida as a walk-on, and by happenstance becomes the starting quarterback because no one was left. Then he takes Florida to its greatest heights and becomes the top passer in the nation. It has to be one of the great success stories in college sports.

Vince Dooley

former 25-year head coach at Georgia,
on the Gators' QB from 1984 through '87

S hane Matthews certainly didn't vault from fifth team in the spring to starter in the fall—with four more experienced quarterbacks ahead of him—because of the system. He proved he could make the system successful. The qualities Shane Matthews has are what you look for in a quarterback.

Steve Spurrier

S purrier said that Shane Matthews was the best quarterback in the history of the university.

Peter Golenbock

> **FAST FACT:** *Spurrier made that comment in 1992, after Matthews's eclipsing of the career UF passing mark set by Kerwin Bell.*

T erry Dean had a gun. He was very confident. He was similar to Coach Spurrier. He was very smart, had great physical attributes, and knew the offense.

Jerome Evans
fullback (1994–96)

Danny was calm. He was cool. He was collected. The team respected him. He made good decisions. He may not have been the most gifted athlete, which isn't to say he wasn't a good athlete, because he was. He was like a coach on the field. He was a student of the game. . . . Danny was a great guy, and he was a great football player, a great talent, a great person. I can't say enough about Danny Wuerffel.

Jerome Evans

They don't make 'em like they used to—except in the case of Danny Wuerffel, who is the mirror-image of coach Steve Spurrier.

Robbie Andreu

The Gainesville Sun, *August 31, 1996*

Steve Spurrier was a very average practice quarterback. If you went to practice and didn't know who he was or who the other quarterbacks were, you wouldn't be sure he was the starter. But on Saturday, he took it up another level. Danny Wuerffel is the same way. When you put the pads on Danny and put him in the clutch, he gets better. In situations where a lot of people get worse, they both got better.

Norm Carlson

You couldn't find a better ambassador for our school. We've known that for four years. Now, everybody knows it.

Jeremy Foley
athletic director (1992–),
on quarterback and 1996 Heisman Trophy
winner Danny Wuerffel

UNIVERSITY OF FLORIDA

Danny Wuerffel

There's nothing phony about him. Danny Wuerffel's the kind of kid you live your whole life hoping your daughter can one day marry. He's sincere, polite, trustworthy, helpful—pretty much all the things they teach you in the Boy Scouts.

Jimmy Ray Stephens
tight end (1973, 1975–76) /
offensive line coach (1993–2001) /
Wuerffel's high school coach in
Ft. Walton Beach

That kid is the best quarterback I've ever seen on any level. No one has ever been that accurate.

Frank Broyles
former Arkansas head football coach
and athletic director,
after witnessing a school record 462-yard,
four-touchdown passing performance
by Danny Wuerffel against the Razorbacks,
October 5, 1996

He's the best quarterback in school history and the best in SEC history. He's got the rings to prove it. No one else has four SEC championship rings.

Steve Spurrier
on Wuerffel

Who could have imagined that the two quarterbacks would end up being similar in such a sensational way, both becoming the school's only Heisman Trophy winners, with one coaching the other?

Peter Kerasotis
writer/author,
on Steve Spurrier and Danny Wuerffel,
both sons of ministers

Every pass Danny threw had 10,000 angels directing and protecting it.

Steve Spurrier
on his talented prodigy, Wuerffel

Danny was simply sensational in big games. I just marveled at how his balls always seemed to get in there by inches. The defender would try to knock it down and would barely miss it, and our guys would catch it. Danny's the best quarterback of all time.

Steve Spurrier
on Wuerffel

There are athletes who are gifted but not competitors, and others who were not as gifted but always seemed to find a way to win. Wuerffel fell into the latter category.

Peter Kerasotis

Doug Johnson, who played professional baseball for the Tampa Bay Devil Rays organization, helped quarterback the Gators to records of 41–8 from 1996 through 1999.

Kevin M. McCarthy

When I broke Coach Spurrier's career passing record, he was very happy for me. He knew his quarterbacks were going to break a lot of his records, just because back when he played they didn't throw the ball that much. He loves for his quarterbacks to break all the records. Danny Wuerffel and I were both ecstatic when Rex Grossman shattered them in 2001. It all comes from the coaching and how he prepares us for the games.

Shane Matthews

He spends more time watching film than some critics at Cannes.

Gene Wojciechowski
*senior national columnist, ESPN.com,
on quarterback Chris Leak*

Throughout the years he's had so much pressure, up and down years. We were so happy to see him in a happy moment like . . . winning the SEC championship. We wanted him to be a quarterback to be remembered. That's how you judge quarterbacks, on championships. For him to get one, he's always going to be remembered.

Andre "Bubba" Caldwell
*wide receiver (2003–07),
on Chris Leak*

I thought Chris Leak was underappreciated all year.

Jim Tressel
Ohio State head coach

He's just the perfect quarterback, your dream quarterback, a once-in-a-lifetime kind of cat.

Opposing high school coach

on record-setting Charlotte, N.C., high school quarterback phenom Chris Leak, who became the second-leading passer in the history of high school sports, throwing for 5,193 yards and 65 touchdowns his senior season alone. Leak led his team, Independence High, to three consecutive state championships

He is officially one of the top two quarterbacks to play at the University of Florida. National championships are how you're judged at Florida.

Urban Meyer

on Chris Leak, joining Danny Wuerffel as the only Gator QBs to win national championships at Florida

Chris Leak

He did what no other Gator except the most exalted ever has done, and a lot more. Danny Wuerffel didn't have to beat invincible Ohio State to win a national championship. He never had to switch to an offense that highlighted his weaknesses in mid-career. He never had to hear thousands of fans drool at the mention of his backup's name. He never had to know that whatever he did, it probably wouldn't be enough. If putting 41 points on the Buckeyes and winning the offensive MVP award isn't enough, Chris Leak should tell people to kiss his championship ring.

David Whitley

Orlando Sentinel

Leak hates to put his head down and pound for yardage; his strengths skew more to reading defenses and delivering pinpoint throws. Tebow, meanwhile, seems to have a physical need for a violent collision every few minutes.

Pat Forde

ESPN.com senior writer

Without two unselfish people, that would have been a problem. And it was a great situation to have all year.

Urban Meyer

on Florida's 2006 two-quarterback setup of senior starter Chris Leak and freshman Tim Tebow

The question was no longer could Leak ever do the things Tebow does. It is now: Can Tebow ever pull a Leak?

David Whitley

following the 2006 national championship game win over Ohio State, in which Leak was named MVP

Doggone it, we want that kid to play. He's a hell of a player.

Urban Meyer

on 2006 freshman quarterback sensation Tim Tebow

Tim Tebow was exactly what Florida needed. The turbo-stud true freshman made the quarterback position a much more immediate running threat, which is the biggest reason why Meyer and Mullen rewarded him with his own package of plays. Having a 235-pound battering ram at your disposal in the red zone and other short-yardage situations is a great luxury.

Pat Forde

Tim Tebow has a linebacker's body and a cheerleader's spirit.

Dave Curtis

Orlando Sentinel *writer*

He's a full-functioning quarterback.

Urban Meyer

on prize 2006 freshman QB Tim Tebow

Tim Tebow continues to impress me with his ability to feel the soft spot of a defense and then do the power running. Just total domination.

Jim Donnan
*former University of Georgia and
Marshall University head coach/
ESPN college football analyst*

Tim Tebow is very similar to Alex Smith. I'm hoping we can do the same things. I expect us to be a bit more option, more quarterback run. A lot of that depends on who our backup is, because you can't jeopardize running Tim as much as he likes to run and as much as we'd like to have him run. I think it will be a little more spread, like we ran at Utah.

Urban Meyer
on utilizing his ace quarterback in 2007

LEGENDS

Wilber Marshall was an omnipresent Goliath. A linebacker that FSU couldn't comb from its blood-stained hair.

Hubert Mizell

St. Petersburg Times, *December 4, 1983, after Marshall and the Florida defense created six turnovers in the 53–14 win over Florida State*

In those days . . . we got the ball to Dale Van Sickel in the flat, and he caught it with great concentration and hands. Then, when the defense moved up to stop that, he would go deep with his tremendous speed and we'd get the easy long-gaining play.

Charley Bachman

Van Sickel made All-American in 1928 partly because of a 1927 play against Washington & Lee. He broke through, took the ball right out of a passer's hand and kept going. It was the kind of spectacular thing the newspapers liked, and it put the spotlight on Van Sickel while we were winning eight in a row and being the national scoring leaders in 1928.

Charley Bachman

Carl Brumbaugh was our passer and our thinker. He could get the ball to Dale Van Sickel. In those days the half-backs passed more than the quarterback. And boy did we pass. In the flats a lot, like they do now. Brumbaugh went on to the Chicago Bears, where he played quarterback for eight years on the great teams with Red Grange and Bronko Nagurski.

Charley Bachman
on the Gator halfback of the 8–1 team
of 1928

He'd have been All-America at a better-known school of the time.

Angus Williams
defensive back (1945, 1948–50),
on teammate and halfback
Charlie Hunsinger

I've said for three years that Charlie Hunsinger is the greatest running back in the league, a truly great ball carrier who doesn't need much in the way of blocking.

Wally Butts

*legendary Georgia head coach,
on UF's two-time All-SEC halfback*

Joe DiMaggio may have been The Yankee Clipper at Yankee Stadium, Stan Musial The Man at Sportsman's Park in St. Louis, and Ted Williams The Splendid Splinter of Fenway Park. But for me, Chuck Hunsinger cast the biggest shadow, along the banks of the St. Johns River, south to the Everglades and north along the Gulf of Mexico to the panhandle.

W. F. Buddy Martin

*author/sportswriter,
on the Gator halfback from 1946 through '49*

Charlie LaPradd was extremely tough. It took two or three men to get him out of the way. They couldn't move him. He was our team captain, and he kept up the spirit on the line. He'd come up and down the line, hitting us on the butt and telling us to get with it and play hard, and we all loved him.

Joe D'Agostino
guard (1951–53),
on UF's All-America tackle of the early 1950s

Charlie LaPradd was well-balanced, powerful, could follow orders, knew his place, was smart, and was a good team player. He did his job. If we had had a whole team of Charlie LaPradds, we'd have won more.

Loren Broadus
halfback (1947–50)

Rick Casares

The stolid, unassuming LaPradd, who had been a paratrooper during World War II, began his football career at Florida after hitchhiking to Gainesville and asking for a chance to play. That he became an All-American was a tribute to his intelligence and desire.

Peter Golenbock

The rest of us were boys, and Rick Casares was a man. At 16, he was New Jersey heavyweight boxing champion. A bad ass. At one time in basketball he held the Coliseum scoring record with 32 points. He was also great in baseball and in track.

Bobby Lance
on the Gators' star fullback of the early 1950s,
who later became a five-time Pro Bowler
with the Chicago Bears

Rick Casares was brilliant. He could carry a 190-pound tackler 10 more yards.

Wally Butts

after Casares rushed 27 times for 108 yards, while kicking three extra points and a 24-yard field goal, in Florida's 30–0 victory over Butts's Bulldogs in 1952

Larry Dupree had the greatest moves I've ever seen in football. I had the ability to hand off to him and look back, and his butt could go sideways faster than it could go forward. He had an instinct for breaking loose and making the big play. Larry Dupree was one of the gutsiest people I ever met in life.

Tom Shannon

quarterback (1962–64)

Larry was one of those players who could stop and start and turn. He had decent size, decent speed, and a lot of agility. He was another natural.

Larry Libertore
quarterback (1960–62),
on Larry Dupree

I had the opportunity to watch the best hips that ever ran for Florida.

Tom Shannon
on three-time All-SEC halfback Larry Dupree

He was probably the best all-around running back I had ever known or seen. He could do it all. He could run and block and catch the ball. He played five years with the Los Angeles Rams. He was a special running back.

Larry Rentz
on three-time All-SEC fullback Larry Smith

Larry Smith was one of the tough guys. He played hard all the time. You knew you had a heck of a player on your football team. Back then kids tried to emulate veteran players who were ahead of them on the team. They literally looked up to them. Larry was the kind of player all good players wanted to be like.

Jack Youngblood

Teammates kidded him, because he spent a lot of time in the weight room getting stronger. He was good, steady, and reliable, but each year he worked harder and harder and harder. He continually improved himself. I thought Jack Youngblood was a good, solid player, but not nearly as good as he turned out to be.

Larry Rentz

I weight trained, which was unheard of back then. Some of my teammates thought I was making a BIG mistake. The [prevailing] concept was that I was going to be a body builder, and I would become muscle-bound and wouldn't be able to move. I designed a weightlifting program for myself that would make me big and strong and fast to play the game.

Jack Youngblood

J ohn Reaves and Carlos Alvarez had big days and got big ink.

Steve Tannen
*cornerback (1967–69),
on UF's record-breaking passing tandem
of 1969*

The thing I liked about Carlos Alvarez, from freshman year on, we'd say, "Let's work on the route tree." Those were all the routes in the playbook. We'd go through every route on both sides of the field, and if it wasn't perfect, either the throw or the route and catch, Carlos would say, "Let's do it again." All I was doing was taking the drop and throwing. He was running his butt off. In 13 years of college and professional football, I never had another end like him. Consequently we got so good that even if he was double or triple covered, we could still connect. It was hard to stop him—hard to stop us. He was brilliant.

John Reaves

Nat Moore is the most dangerous back I have ever coached.

Doug Dickey

quarterback (1951–53)/
head coach (1970–78),
on the Gator running back of 1972 and '73,
later an All-Pro wide receiver with the
Miami Dolphins

He was the most complete back I have seen in the SEC, a picture back. If we drew on a blackboard what we wanted in a back, it would come out Nat Moore.

Vince Dooley

Jimmy DuBose was a legitimate superstar. He was the best wishbone fullback in the country. Jimmy was a tremendous runner, a great blocker, unselfish, could catch, would do it all. He was the heart and soul of the team.

Don Gaffney

quarterback (1973–75),
on the mid-'70s fullback

Wes Chandler, who is on UF's Team of the Century as a wide receiver, led the team in receptions three years (1975–1977). He was a first-team All-American for two years (1976, 1977) and still holds the school record for career yards per reception (21.3 on 92 catches). He later played in the NFL for the New Orleans Saints (1978–1981), San Diego Chargers (1982–1987), and 49ers (1988).

Kevin M. McCarthy

Wes was Wes, an All-American, a tremendous big playmaker. In 1975 he came into his own and gained national prominence as a wide receiver.

Don Gaffney

At outside linebacker, Wilber Marshall became a force, a two-time All-American, a three-time All-SEC player, and a first-round NFL draft pick, going to the Chicago Bears, where he was part of that great 1985 Super Bowl championship team. In 1992, he played on another Super Bowl winner with the Washington Redskins.

Peter Kerasotis

I tried to cater my game after certain players. I liked Dick Butkus because he was nasty. I liked the way Mike Singletary played because he was nasty and an intelligent player. Willie Lanier the same way. Those were guys, when I was growing up, I'd look at and say, "That's me."

Wilber Marshall

Wilber Marshall

T hroughout his career he was known as a hard-nosed, ferocious—if not vicious—player.

Peter Kerasotis
on early '80s linebacker Wilber Marshall

L inebackers aren't supposed to get there in time. But Marshall did. He messed up our passing game and our running game. We tried to run sweeps to the side opposite him, and he would come from clear off the backside and make a tackle behind the line of scrimmage before the runner could turn upfield. I have never seen anybody quick enough to do that.

Bruce Matthews
former Southern Cal All-America guard/
NFL Hall of Famer,
on Marshall's 14-tackle (nine solo), four-sack
performance in Florida's 17–9 win over USC
in 1982

J ohn L. Williams is probably the best athlete on the team. He has power and speed to the outside, which most fullbacks don't have, and he has great hands.

Kerwin Bell
quarterback (1984–87)

I 've always said I like to catch passes and then run over some people.

John L. Williams
fullback (1982–85),
after catching six passes for 72 yards
and tallying 110 rushing yards against
Kentucky, November 18, 1984

H e reads the holes and explodes through them.

Bob Sims
offensive lineman (1986–87),
on freshman running back sensation
Emmitt Smith, in 1987

Emmitt Smith

Trying to pin down exactly what made him so extraordinary was like trying to put your finger on a drop of mercury.

Peter Kerasotis
on Emmitt Smith

He has great vision, great balance. You seldom get a clear shot at him.

Galen Hall
on Emmitt Smith

I'd like to win two or three Heismans.

Emmitt Smith
running back (1987–89)

That was one of Errict Rhett's biggest games. He was a workhorse. We were just pounding him for three or four yards at a time, and he just kept going.

Terry Dean
on the big back's 41 carries and 183 rushing yards against Georgia in the 1993 downpour at Jacksonville

Jacquez Green

Ike Hilliard (1994–96) was a phenomenal player. He combined great speed, size, and was very physical. He had big legs, and he was not afraid to run into guys and make things happen.

Danny Wuerffel

Jacquez Green was the smoothest, fastest guy you'll see. He could run the 40 in 4.4, and it looked like he was jogging. He doesn't give the impression he's running fast, but he is, and it's one of the reasons he's so hard to cover.

Danny Wuerffel

As a punt returner, Jacquez Green holds school records for a single season (392 yards on 27 returns in 1997) and for most touchdowns in a career (4).

Kevin M. McCarthy

LEGENDARY COACHES

rban Meyer showed without question he is one of the top three college coaches in America. If Nick Saban is worth $4 million, Meyer is worth five. He not only outcoached The Sweater, he actually has outdone The Visor. It took Spurrier seven years to win a national title; it's taken Meyer two.

Mike Bianchi

Gator Mentors

Everyone in the Western Hemisphere is familiar with the phenomenal success of the Florida football program under former head coach Steve Spurrier, and now the cloud-parting Second Gator Coming under Urban Meyer.

But only the truest die-hard fans of Gator history are likely conversant with the quality coaching contributions generated by early mentors Tom Sebring, Major James A. Van Fleet, Charley Bachman, and Bob Woodruff.

The Ray Graves era in particular, during the decade of the 1960s, helped put the Gators on the national map. It's no coincidence that UF's first Heisman Trophy winner was also spawned during that upbeat period. And let's not forget the brilliant five-year run in the mid- to late-1980s of Galen Hall, who set the stage for the magnificence of the '90s.

All in all, it adds up to some serious Gator mentoring.

H e was a total gentleman, and I have been associated with the best— Knute Rockne, Bob Zuppke, Stagg, Warner—and none were any better than Tom Sebring.

Nash Higgins
*assistant coach under Sebring,
UF's head coach from 1925 through '27*

A t halftime, Coach Woodruff would turn to the board, take another look, turn around to us, give us that little grin of his and yell, "and don't forget to Oski Wow Wow!" He'd do it every time. And we'd leap up and yell, "Oski Wow Wow!"

Charlie LaPradd
*defensive tackle (1950–52),
Woodruff's quirky phrase was derived from one
of Tennessee head coach Gen. Robert Neyland's
favorite words: "Oski." Woodruff was a Volunteer
player (1936–38) under Neyland*

Woodruff, with his long periods of silence, would make you wonder if he was 30 minutes ahead of you or 30 minutes behind.

Charlie LaPradd

I was the oratorical equivalent of a blocked punt.

Bob Woodruff

whose self-deprecating assessment, based on his inability to speak well in public and to rarely come to the point in press-related matters, belied his solid contributions to the UF program in his decade as head coach. Woodruff raised Florida football to new levels within the SEC, including two third-place finishes

In his first three years, he had been beaten 63–14 and 46–15, been 0–5 at one point, had oranges thrown at him at his old home place of Knoxville, been cussed, discussed, helped, hurt, bad-mouthed by some of his own players, praised by others, been through injuries to his best people, seen student ticket prices raised, seen athletes try to union-ize on campus, had had players quit and come back, or just quit; and had even fallen down stairs while on crutches recovering from a knee operation from an old football injury sustained as a Florida player. But Doug Dickey had not just survived; he was quietly building a stable program that he had promised.

Tom McEwen

He allowed black players to be themselves. He was really a good man, a wonderful man, and a hell of a recruiter. Every time we talked to a kid who he wanted, we'd say, "Hey, man, Coach Dickey is wonderful." That's why Florida signed so many good players.

Don Gaffney

Charley Pell had the most profound effect of anybody in UF history next to Steve Spurrier. Charley Pell made Steve Spurrier's job a good one.

Bill Carr
center (1964–66)/
UF athletic director (1980–86)

The Lord is good to those who have great defensive tackles.

Charley Pell

I walked into my office and put the key in the door, and it still worked. When it doesn't work, I'll know I'm no longer the coach.

Charley Pell
terminated as head coach after three games of the 1984 season for a myriad of NCAA violations

There's probably two legacies. There's the negative one, the troubles we had. But you can't judge his whole life on that. He taught us how to work, what it takes to compete on this level in terms of facilities and commitment. Part of his legacy will be the NCAA situation, but there's certainly a lot more positives beyond that.

Jeremy Foley
on the turbulent head coaching reign of Charley Pell

Charley Pell cared more about his players than any coach I ever played for.

Robin Fisher
nose guard (1979–81)

When I think of Galen Hall back at Penn State in 1959, I think of one of the really great players we have ever had at Penn State; probably the smartest football player I have ever been around in the 35 years I've been at Penn State. . . . Galen is solid, poised, knows what it takes to win, and understands the things important to the integrity of the university.

Joe Paterno
*legendary Penn State head coach,
on his former quarterback, in 1986,
then head coach at Florida*

There probably isn't a better "X and O" coach in college football. He knows the game, knows how to attack defenses and always has the calm and presence of mind to be able to think under pressure during the course of the game. He is a great Saturday coach.

Gil Brandt

*former Dallas Cowboys general manager,
on former head coach Galen Hall*

Steve Spurrier's system is like nothing college football has seen, standing out like a computer among cavemen.

Dan LeBatard

ESPN the Magazine

Steve has THE offensive mind. He is the master of the unexpected and he is the master at creating mismatches. Nobody does it better.

Terry Donahue

*former UCLA head coach,
on Spurrier*

Steve and I were roommates on the road. From the first, I saw that Steve had a very, very good sense of values. He's very compassionate and extremely family oriented. He's as honest as the day is long—he would never cheat at recruiting, and he can't stand to be cheated against.

Tom Shannon

Steve is playing a different type of football. It's not the same game he grew up with or I grew up with. I don't believe the other coaches have caught up with it. Any time you put that many points on the board, it's something remarkable.

Otis Boggs
longtime Gators broadcaster

He draws up his ball plays in the all-business manner of personal checks, each of them worth six points, and then is genuinely shocked if they should bounce.

Dave George
Palm Beach Post *columnist,*
on Steve Spurrier

He was always giving you things to think about. Our playbook was filled with poems and quotes from literature or on Vince Lombardi or John Wooden—things he wanted you to think about. When you're 19 and you read them, you go, "Whatever. Throw me the damn ball." But as you get older, you begin to understand what they are trying to instill in you.

Paul Bowen
on Steve Spurrier

He's a phenomenal coach; a very funny man. He does things differently from any other coach I've ever seen. He doesn't over-labor, doesn't work hundreds of hours. He doesn't take it overly serious when other people do. Yet at the same time he's incredibly intense, a perfectionist in many ways.

Danny Wuerffel

on Steve Spurrier

Steve Spurrier is the best quarterback coach in all of football—pros, college, junior high, Little League, anywhere. Steve Spurrier is, bar none, the best offensive coach in the country.

Lee Corso

former Indiana University head coach,
current ESPN college football analyst

Steve Spurrier

Coach Spurrier really understands what you are going through and what you are seeing on the practice field and on game days. He has a tremendous ability to transfer his knowledge to you. It's not that he knows so much that makes him special to a quarterback. What's special is that he will teach you what he knows, and a lot of coaches can't do that.

Danny Wuerffel

I don't think you should measure a coaching staff by whether it puts in more hours than everybody they go against. Measure it by what gets done while it's working. Some staffs work too much and come up with bad ideas because they're dead tired.

Steve Spurrier

1991

purrier is every bit as much a quarterback today as when he won the 1966 Heisman Trophy at Florida. The high-flying Gators attack is his offense. He knows what to do when the pocket is crumbling and options one through three are covered. That's one of the reasons why Spurrier has had fine quarterbacks wherever he's coached.

Michael Bradley
Bob Griese's 1996 College Football

e had the capability of adlibbing during the course of a game better than anybody I'd ever been around, or have been around since.

Cris Collinsworth
on Steve Spurrier

he Steve Spurrier passing system is years ahead of modern science in cloning.

Mike Lopresti
USA TODAY

If you want to write a history of football's offensive formations, get a Florida playbook. In watching film of Florida, you are watching the most sophisticated offense and passing attack in college football. Steve Spurrier is simply a brilliant offensive coach.

Lou Holtz

former head coach at Arkansas, Minnesota, Notre Dame, and South Carolina

I really have accepted a philosophy or theory that you can't listen to the enemies. You can't listen to the Gator-haters. Everybody is not going to love the Gators. Everybody is not going to love me. I say things a little differently than most coaches do. But I'm honest and I call them like I see them.

Steve Spurrier

We won't get a big head because Coach Spurrier won't let us.

Ike Hilliard

wide receiver (1994–96),
on the Gators' No. 1 ranking during their
1996 national championship season

He believes in us and we believe in him.

Terence Barber

wide receiver (1988–90),
on Steve Spurrier

It's fun coaching at Florida. I don't think all the gold in Fort Knox could get me to go to the NFL.

Steve Spurrier

November 18, 1990

FAST FACT: *Spurrier would opt for a $25 million, five-year contract with the Washington Redskins in 2002, exiting the NFL after just two seasons and a less-than-sterling 12–20 worksheet.*

Golf season is a lot longer for college coaches than it is for the pro coaches.

Steve Spurrier
on NCAA restrictions outlawing year-round recruiting

I would like to be remembered as a coach whose teams were always in the hunt. We didn't win them all, but we were up there fighting for it. It didn't work out all the time, but we came close about every time.

Steve Spurrier

He's not afraid to go against the grain. He's a risk-taker, and he's making a living right now doing it. He's doing things other coaches are scared to do.

Andre Caldwell
on Urban Meyer

MAJOR
MOMENTS

That has to be one of the greatest football games ever as far as momentum
shifts.

Urban Meyer

*on the 2006 SEC Championship Game win
over Arkansas, a wild affair that saw the
Razorbacks fight back from a 17–0 deficit to take
the lead, only to eventually bow to Florida,
38–28. In the game, three touchdown passes
were thrown by someone other than the
quarterback (two by the Hogs)*

Lightning in a jar

Attempting to cram all the great moments in Florida's illustrious gridiron history into one chapter is like trying to catch all the fireflies in the sky in a little glass jar.

Yet any moment still ringing with fond remembrance is worth the time to reflect upon: the stunning upset of Alabama in 1923; posting Boston College's only loss on its otherwise perfect 1939 slate; an unexpected win over Georgia in the doldrums of the "Golden Era;" Spurrier's Heisman-clinching outing vs. Auburn in 1966; Larry Smith's 94-yard TD run in the '67 Orange Bowl; Reaves-to-Alvarez in the 1969 record-smashing debut of the two soph phenoms; beating Tennessee in the '69 Gator Bowl; James Jones's one-handed grab that killed the 'Canes in 1982, Kerwin Bell's courageous performance against Auburn in '86, the multitude of highlights throughout the 1990s, the second national title in 2006 . . .

On second thought, better punch some more air holes in that lightning-bug jar.

The Crimson Tide has been turned into the "thin dripping red line," banners of blood and white are at half-mast in the city by the steel mills, and the "Fighting Gators" of Florida have returned triumphant to the homeland after a brilliant season of play. . . . Alabama was game but beaten. Like Arabs, they folded their tents in the night and with heavy hearts returned to the Capstone.

The Gainesville Sun

November 29, 1923,
after Florida's stunning 16–6 upset of
Alabama in Birmingham

T he highlight of coach Josh Cody's years at Florida was taking on undefeated Boston College under a new coach, a man named Frank Leahy, in 1939. Leahy lost only one regular-season game in his two years at BC, that to those underdog Gators from Florida, 7–0. Leahy even started his second string. It was a mistake. . . . Boston's offense, led by sensational Charlie O'Rourke, was stopped eight times inside the Gator 15, and six of those times Fergie Ferguson was responsible for the game-saving play. His performance that day would have to rank with any in Florida history for sheer single-handed, effective, defensive heroics.

Tom McEwen

Spurrier kicks way to Heisman

In 1966, Florida quarterback Steve Spurrier created enough miracles through six games to be given serious consideration by the nation's media for the country's highest collegiate football award.

In Game 7, tough rival Auburn tied the Gators at 27–27 with just over four minutes left. UF began its final drive at their own 26. A Spurrier-to-Richard Trapp pass play followed a roughing penalty against the Tigers, placing the ball on the Auburn 40. Florida moved down to the Tiger 20 on a flare pass with 2:42 remaining. But on the next play, Spurrier, rushed hard, was flagged for intentional grounding, now making it second and 29 from the Auburn 39. A reception over the middle by John Coons took UF down to the 24. After a dropped pass, the Gators faced fourth and 14.

Spurrier, not Florida's regular kicker, then lined up for a 40-yard field goal try. The kick was straight, high, and long. As the ball cleared the crossbar, UF fans erupted. He had done it again. Improbably, the surprising Gators were 7–0, and Spurrier, finding yet one more way to win, surpassed Purdue's Bob Griese as the leading Heisman candidate.

Steve Spurrier boots a 40-yard, game-winning field goal against Auburn in 1966.

Florida 30, Auburn 27. The game. The one first thought of when Steve Spurrier's legend is discussed.

Peter Kerasotis

I had heard before the game that Steve told some players during breakfast that he dreamed he kicked a field goal to beat Auburn.

Ray Graves
on Steve Spurrier's prophetic vision before his legendary 40-yard field goal to beat the Tigers, 30–27, in 1966, cementing the Heisman Trophy for the UF quarterback

My only surprise is that he hasn't done it before.

Ed Kensler
assistant coach (1964–69), on Larry Smith's 94-yard touchdown burst against Georgia Tech in the 1967 Orange Bowl

Larry Smith's 94-yard Orange Bowl TD Run

He was only a sophomore but his contribution to the winning Gators' 1967 Orange Bowl performance was Oscar worthy.

Late in the third quarter, running back Larry Smith ran inside tackle then suddenly burst into an open field, blazing down the sidelines for a walloping 94-yard touchdown dash that powered Florida to a 27–12 victory over Georgia Tech and netted Smith—caught most of the season in the long shadow of Heisman Trophy-winning teammate Steve Spurrier—the 1967 Orange Bowl Classic Outstanding Player trophy.

"I really had no idea I could go that far," said Smith, who totaled 187 yards rushing.

"Smith's a helluva player," said end Paul Ewaldsen. "He can block, he can catch. He oughta win the Heisman in two years."

Heisman winner Spurrier concurred. "He's in a class by himself in the Southeastern Conference," admitted the Gators' star QB. "If he continues, he'll be up in New York in two years to get that Heisman award."

Smith of course didn't fail to credit others. "Graham McKeel and Ewaldsen did the key blocks," he said. "All I had to do was run."

L et me tell you about one run that Richard Trapp made. If you haven't seen it, get the tape. This was literally a 5-yard pass. Trapp then ran from one side of the field to the other. He ran from right to left and then back toward the middle. The play went for 52 yards and a touchdown. All the players and coaches were watching the film, and there were something like nine Georgia players who had a shot at him. It is still the single most unbelievable run I have ever seen.

Larry Rentz

on Trapp's legendary catch and run through the Bulldogs during a 17–16 victory in 1967

I will never forget it. Offensive coordinator Fred Pancoast stood up and told us, "We are going to score on the third play of the game." We went, "Right, right." Houston kicked the ball back to us. John Reaves got the ball. He threw down and out to Carlos Alvarez. Again he threw down and out to Carlos. And we scored on the third play!

Jack Youngblood
*on UF's shocking upset of No. 1-ranked
Houston, 59–34, in the 1969 season opener—
the collegiate debut of Reaves and Alvarez*

This morning John Reaves—the now famous No. 7 on the University of Florida football team—is to Gator grid fans what oranges are to the citrus industry. Reaves broke in with the most fantastic explosion in Florida football history.

Jim McDonald

Orlando Sentinel, *September 21, 1969,*
after the Gator sophomore quarterback's
record-smashing performance in his first-ever
collegiate start, in which he threw five
touchdown passes in a 59–34 devastation
of Houston

I t was the greatest block of them all.

Steve Tannen

*on his first-quarter block of a Tennessee punt
recovered in the UT end zone by Gator
linebacker Mike Kelley to give UF a 7–0 lead
in the 1969 Gator Bowl. It was Tannen's
seventh blocked punt in two years.
Florida won the game, 14–13, to close out
the Ray Graves era at UF*

I t's one of the greatest moments in
University of Florida football history.

Ray Graves

*on Florida's 12–8 upset win over Auburn
at Jordan-Hare Stadium in 1973. The Gators'
offense revolved around the robust running
of tailback Vince Kendrick and the sprintout
passing and running of sophomore QB
Don Gaffney in his first-ever start for UF*

I t was the greatest catch I've ever seen . . . a Willie Mays deluxe catch.

Charley Pell

*on fullback James Jones's leaping reception
from quarterback Wayne Peace with just 1:48
remaining to defeat Miami, 17–14, in the
1982 season opener, the Gators' first win over
the Hurricanes in five years*

W hen I went down I thought I had gone out of bounds and didn't think it was a touchdown . . . When I saw the official signal touchdown, I looked down and was surprised to see I was over the goal.

James Jones

*fullback (1979–82),
on his game-winning TD reception, caught
in a crowd at the Miami goal line in 1982.
The catch beat the Hurricanes, 17–14*

The University of Florida captured probably the greatest victory in the school's 76-year-old football history here Saturday afternoon, holding off vaunted, mighty Southern Cal at the gun, 17–9.

Jack Hairston

Gainesville Sun *sports editor,*
September 12, 1982

If I've seen a better quarterback, I don't know when. It has to be one of the finest comebacks ever.

Galen Hall

after witnessing Kerwin Bell's gutsy
performance in the memorable fourth-quarter
18-point comeback victory over Auburn,
November 2, 1986. Down 17–0 in the final
quarter, an injured Bell came off the bench to
run for a touchdown, throw for another,
plus run in the critical two-point conversion
try that won the game with just
36 seconds remaining

That's why people play this game. An athlete loves to win a game, to come back like we did is the highest high you can have.

Kerwin Bell

*after his last-quarter heroics gave UF a
stunning 18–17 win over Auburn in 1986*

This is something you savor. The SEC title has been a long time in coming, and it's a great victory for the other guys (former players) who didn't get the opportunity.

Willie Jackson Sr.

*wide receiver (1970–72),
on the Gators' first official conference crown
in 1991. Jackson's son, Willie Jr., was a member
of that title squad*

One great thing: I never lost at Florida Field. I will always cherish that.

Shane Matthews

I came over to the sideline. I was like, "Coach, I don't think they can stop me tonight."

Errict Rhett

after the first few plays of the 1994 Sugar Bowl, in which the Gators ultimately trounced West Virginia 41–7, behind Rhett's 105 yards rushing and career-high three touchdowns

This is the way I wanted to go out. I will always remember this game, my last game as a Gator.

Errict Rhett

following his MVP performance in the 1994 Sugar Bowl win over West Virginia

This was different from any game Florida ever played. It was Spurrier's finest moment. If you never believed in him before, you have to now. Saturday's 62–37 victory over Tennessee was perhaps the most amazing game ever played at Florida Field, a symphony of offense that left the 85,105 breathless.

Pat Dooley
Gainesville Sun *columnist, September 17, 1995*

UF fell behind Peyton Manning and an unstoppable Vol offense 30–14 in the first half, as a silent crowd looked on in gloom. But in perhaps the most impressive offensive performance of the Steve Spurrier era, the Gators overwhelmed UT with a 48–0 blitz, the most points allowed by the Vols since 1893.

Robbie Andreu
September 17, 1995

Catching four touchdowns is something you dream about, but it wasn't just me. We played hard and smart in a big game.

Ike Hilliard

who scored four times on nine receptions for 112 yards in the Gators' 62–37 splattering of the Big Orange, September 16, 1995

Back-to-back. Three minutes apart. His two winding, cutting, historic runs across Florida Field for touchdowns on consecutive punt returns in the third quarter tied the NCAA record for punt returns for touchdowns in a game and tied the Florida season record.

Robbie Andreu

on Jacquez Green's record-setting performance in the 65–0 ravaging of Kentucky in 1996

That was a phenomenal day for him. There were some really incredible moves he made. He looked like he was trapped, and he went backwards, and sideways, and forward, and I stood on the stands watching him just like any other spectator, watching his amazing plays. [The first punt return was for 66 yards, the second for 79.] On the second touchdown, he probably ran 200 yards.

Danny Wuerffel

on Jacquez Green's career day, in the 65–0 obliteration of Kentucky in 1996, in which the Gator star took back a pair of consecutive third-period punt returns for touchdowns on long, broken-field runs within a three-minute span

L ong tweaked as the only one of Florida's Big Three college football programs without a national championship, the Florida Gators finally stormed the crown room Thursday night. They blasted in with a Shotgun.

Larry Guest

Orlando Sentinel, *January 4, 1997,*
on Florida's first national championship—
a 52–20 drubbing of archrival FSU in the
1997 Sugar Bowl, sparked by Gator
quarterback Danny Wuerffel's throwing from
a deep set

T hose Orange-and-Blue faithful convinced that God is a Gator can point to new evidence provided in recent weeks.

Larry Guest

Orlando Sentinel, *January 4, 1997,*
after Florida's improbable run through a
maze of mathematical possibilities that had
to happen for them to play FSU
for the 1996 national championship

od gave us a mulligan.

Steve Spurrier

on the turn of events that transpired, enabling Florida to gain the 1996 national crown. Having lost to Florida State in late regular season, the Gators set about rebounding by beating Alabama in the SEC championship game, then watched as Texas upset third-ranked Nebraska in the Big 12 Conference title game, followed by Ohio State's upset of No. 2 Arizona State in the Rose Bowl, thus setting up an improbable rematch of FSU and Florida for the national title in the Sugar Bowl

If we were going to beat Florida again, we had to get to Danny Wuerffel, and we just couldn't.

Bobby Bowden

Florida State head coach,
after the 1996 national championship game
loss to Florida. In the teams' earlier encounter
to close the regular season, FSU had beaten
UF, 24–21, and beaten Wuerffel to a pulp.
But the Gators' offensive line protected the
Heisman Trophy-winning quarterback in the
title game in New Orleans, as Florida gained
revenge with a 52–20 pounding of the No. 1
Seminoles. UF's 32-point victory margin was
the largest over a top-ranked team in
NCAA history

T hat hasn't happened around here in a long time. To accomplish something like that, that's a big statement for Florida football.

Andre Caldwell

*following Florida's 25–19 victory over
Vanderbilt and a Tennessee loss to LSU
to clinch the 2006 SEC Eastern Division
championship, the Gators' first since 2000*

I 'm so happy to be a Gator.

Jarvis Moss

*defensive end (2005–06),
who deflected a low field-goal attempt with
eight seconds left to preserve Florida's 17–16
victory over South Carolina in 2006. Moss
also blocked a fourth-quarter extra point that
accounted for the final
winning margin*

I knew we had Moss. I know how hard those guys work [on field-goal blocks].

Chris Leak

*on the field-goal block by Jarvis Moss
to seal UF's big 2006 win over
the Gamecocks*

He's a freak.

Urban Meyer

*on 6–6 kick-blocking defensive end
Jarvis Moss, possessor of a 40-inch
vertical leap*

That kid could block a kick on anyone.

Steve Spurrier

*South Carolina head coach,
following Moss's one-man ambush of his
Gamecocks, November 11, 2006*

C hris Leak just said, "Let's go win this game. Let's end this season 11–1. Let's end it right here on this drive."

Andre Caldwell

on Florida's game-winning early fourth-quarter drive at Doak Campbell Stadium, November 26, 2006, to top FSU for UF's third consecutive victory against the Seminoles. The Gators also posted their fourth 11-win season in school history. Caldwell finished with eight catches for 124 yards in the 21–14 win

I t's here. We are going to go play for a ring in Atlanta.

Urban Meyer

following his Gators' 21–14 victory over in-state rival Florida State in 2006 before heading to the SEC Championship Game against Arkansas

I t was definitely motivation. We wanted to go out and finish off the game.

Percy Harvin

on the news within the Gators' Georgia Dome locker room during halftime of the 2006 SEC Championship Game against Arkansas that No. 2 Southern California had been knocked out of the BCS National Championship Game by a 13–9 upset loss to UCLA. The freshman Harvin, MVP in Florida's 38–28 win over the No. 8 Razorbacks, scored two touchdowns, as the Gators also tallied off a blocked punt and a botched return to take its first SEC crown since 2000

After Arkansas stormed ahead, 21–17, Florida reclaimed the momentum when Reggie Fish made a ghastly error on a punt return. Filling in for the Razorbacks' regular returner, who didn't make the trip because of an injury, Fish inexplicably tried to field a punt near his own goal line with an over-the-shoulder catch. He couldn't hang on, the ball squirted into the end zone, and Wondy Pierre-Louis fell on it to put the Gators back ahead.

ESPN.com news services

*on the turning point in UF's 2006
SEC Championship Game win over Arkansas*

Florida beat Michigan on Sunday in the only game that mattered.

Associated Press

following the Gators' SEC title-game win over Arkansas. The next day it was announced that No. 4 Florida had been extended the invitation to play Ohio State in the BCS National Championship Game rather than idle No. 3 Michigan, which had lost to the Buckeyes to close out the regular season. Helping the Gators leapfrog over the competition was UCLA's upset of No. 2 Southern Cal

Chris Leak capped UF's first-half scoring with a 37-yard strike to Percy Harvin, pushing the advantage to 17–0 over Arkansas. Leak became Florida's all-time leader in passing yards on the play, breaking Danny Wuerffel's career record of 10,875.

gatorzone.com
during the 2006 SEC title game

A Tebow run was as sure as the UT band belting out "Rocky Top." Meyer knew it, the 100,000-some fans there knew it, and the 11 Vols defenders knew it.

Dave Curtis

on Tim Tebow's 2-yard run on fourth-and-1 from the Tennessee 28, midway through the fourth quarter in Knoxville, down six points. Tebow gained two and the Gators scored the winning touchdown two plays later, beginning a run of seven SEC wins in eight conference contests in 2006

W e all believed in him, and we all believed in that play.

Drew Miller

right guard (2004–07), on the big fourth down play supplied by Tim Tebow that ignited Florida's 21–20 come-from-behind victory over the Vols in 2006

I remember before the play, the head referee came over to me and said, "Do you believe? This is really crazy."

Tim Tebow

quarterback (2006–),
before the fourth-and-1 play at the UT 28
midway through the final quarter of the 2006
Florida-Tennessee game in Knoxville.

O ur speed was too much for them. That's why we're national champions.

Ray McDonald

defensive end (2003–06),
on the Gators' 2006 national championship
victory over heavily favored Ohio State in
Florida's 100th season of college football

ou can't even put it into words. It's just so special.

Tim Tebow

*following Florida's 2006 BCS
National Championship Game whipping
of previously undefeated and top-ranked
Ohio State, 41–14. The vaunted freshman
QB threw one touchdown pass and powered
in for another score*

can't say enough about those guys. They came out and they fought. They did all the things they needed to do to win.

Troy Smith

*Ohio State's Heisman Trophy-winning
quarterback,
after the Buckeyes' crushing loss to UF in
the 2006 national title game. Smith was a
dismal 4-of-14 for 35 yards passing with one
interception. Florida sacked him five times,
holding him to minus-29 yards on 10 runs
in the rout*

hris Leak humiliated Mr. Heisman. To say he won the personal matchup with Troy Smith is like saying Sitting Bull got the best of Custer.

Pat Forde

t was probably the most dominating football game I've every seen. I've seen a lot of dominating games. I've been in a few—just ask Florida State.

Danny Wuerffel
on the Gators' rout of Ohio State in the 2006 BCS National Championship Game

This national championship game win completes a rainbow career arc for Leak, splashing him down in a pot of gold in his final college game. This was the day Florida fans envisioned when the nation's No. 1 high school quarterback in 2002 committed to the Gators.

Pat Forde

after the 41–14 conquest of Ohio State for the 2006 national crown

It just shows with hard work anything's possible. This is the best moment of my life.

Derrick Harvey

defensive end (2005–),
following UF's 2006 national title-tilt win
over the Buckeyes, in which Harvey was
named defensive MVP

My legacy was to get University of Florida football back here [to the national championship game]. And with my teammates and coaches, we were able to do that.

Chris Leak

It hit me out there, being around my teammates one last time. It was a great feeling. It's really going to hit me when I go off and return after a couple years and I still see 2006 national champs on that stadium wall. That's going to mean a lot to me; all the sacrifice and hard work that myself, my coaches, my teammates, my family put in.

Chris Leak
at the celebration ceremony in Gainesville
after UF's 2006 title game victory over
Ohio State

THE FLORIDA GATORS ALL-TIME TEAM

*D*anny Wuerffel, Cris Collinsworth, Trace Armstrong, Kevin Carter, Larry Smith, Larry Dupree, Lito Sheppard, Fred Taylor, Chris Leak, Shane Matthews, Ike Hilliard, Reidel Anthony—and those are just some of the players who didn't make it! The irony of every all-time team is that those not selected are often more conspicuous than those legends chosen.

Wuerffel sitting on the pine? Simple. He had the only other Gator Heisman Trophy winner, and one of the finest coaches in college football history, on the sideline, mentoring him. Spurrier, on the other hand, as a player, was allowed unprecedented freedom on the field, a future coaching genius in the making. Both were consummate winners, but Spurrier's overall athleticism as a quality punter and clutch field-goal kicker gives him the edge.

Florida Gators All-Time Team

OFFENSE

Carlos Alvarez, *wide receiver*
Wes Chandler, *wide receiver*
Lomas Brown, *tackle*
Guy Dennis, *guard*
Bill Carr, *center*
Jeff Zimmerman, *guard*
Jason Odom, *tackle*
Jack Jackson, *wide receiver*
Steve Spurrier, *quarterback*
Emmitt Smith, *running back*
Errict Rhett, *running back*

DEFENSE

Jack Youngblood, *defensive end*
Charlie LaPradd, *defensive tackle*
Brad Culpepper, *defensive tackle*
Alex Brown, *defensive end*
Wilber Marshall, *linebacker*
David Little, *linebacker*
Jevon Kearse, *linebacker*
Steve Tannen, *defensive back*
Fred Weary, *defensive back*
Louis Oliver, *defensive back*
Jarvis Williams, *defensive back*
Ray Criswell, *punter*
Judd Davis, *kicker*
Jacquez Green, *punt/kick returner*

Steve Spurrier, *coach*

CARLOS ALVAREZ
Flankerback (1969–71)

Consensus All-American (1969),
All-SEC (1969),
Academic All-America Hall of Fame (1989)

The greatest pass-catcher I've ever had at Florida.

Ray Graves

on Carlos Alvarez before his college debut against Houston in 1969. In that game Alvarez caught six receptions for 182 yards and two touchdowns, including a 70-yard bomb from fellow soph John Reaves on the third play of the game. Alvarez's receiving yardage exceeded the previous Florida single-game all-time high set by Richard Trapp against Georgia in 1967

WES CHANDLER
Split end (1974–77)
All-American (1976, '77),
All-SEC (1976, '77)

I 've always thought Wes was the best receiver ever at Florida. He had the tremendous speed, the great hands, and the power to break tackles. It's unfortunate that he played in a system that didn't get him the ball. He never had the advantage of a passer like John Reaves to throw him the ball or a system that took full advantage of his skills.

Carlos Alvarez

LOMAS BROWN
Tackle (1981–84)
Consensus All-American (1984), All-SEC (1984), Jacobs Blocking Trophy (SEC's top blocker, 1984)

We had more talent than anybody in the country. . . . I mean Lomas Brown, our tackle, is STILL playing with the New York Giants. I don't know how it's possible. He's just doing it.

Bob Hewko
quarterback (1980–82),
in 2001

FAST FACT: Brown, a member of the "Great Wall of Florida," played 18 years in the NFL and was a seven-time Pro Bowler.

GUY DENNIS
Guard (1966–68)
All-American (1968), All-SEC (1967, '68)

The highest grading lineman ever in University of Florida history.

Alpha Eta Chapter History

BILL CARR
Center (1964–66)
All-American (1966), All-SEC (1966)

O ffensive captain of 1967 Orange Bowl team. Started 32 consecutive games at center earning All-America honors his senior season. Played in 1967 Senior Bowl. Drafted by New Orleans Saints but ROTC commitment resulted in his entering U.S. Army, where he served in Korea. UF athletic director (1980–86).

2006 University of Florida Football Guide

JEFF ZIMMERMAN
Guard (1983–86)
All-American (1985, '86), All-SEC (1985, '86)

H e became the first non-senior offensive lineman in school history to garner first team All-America honors (Walter Camp Football Foundation, Sporting News, 1985).The first offensive lineman in school history to be named first team All-America in two seasons (Walter Camp Foundation, 1986).

2006 University of Florida Football Guide

JASON ODOM

Tackle (1992–95)

Consensus All-American (1995), All-SEC (1994, '95), Jacobs Blocking Trophy winner (1994, '95)

Named to virtually every first team All-America team (1995). Named the recipient of the Jacobs Blocking Trophy as the SEC's premier blocker for second straight year in 1995, the first player since 1982 to capture the award in back-to-back years. A four-year starter who played in 49 games with 46 starts.

2006 University of Florida Football Guide

JACK JACKSON

Wide receiver (1992–94)

Consensus All-American (1994), All-SEC (1994), SEC Offensive Player of the Year (*Football News*, 1994)

Jack Jackson was fearless, had super speed, ran really good routes, and would get open and get to the ball. You put it there, and he was going to get it.

Terry Dean

STEVE SPURRIER
Quarterback (1964–66)

Heisman Trophy winner (1966),
consensus All-American (1966),
All-SEC (1965, '66),
SEC Player of the Year (1966),
Sugar Bowl MVP (1966),
College Football Hall of Fame (1986)

He's unreal. Sometimes I just can't get over the things Steve Spurrier does with a football. I've seen a lot of college quarterbacks and he is the best I've ever seen.

Ray Graves

Spurrier, with his hands tied behind his back and facing a firing squad, would be favored to escape.

John Logue
Atlanta Journal

EMMITT SMITH

Running back (1987–89)

Consensus All-American (1989),
All-SEC (1987–89),
SEC Player of the Year (1989),
National Freshman of the Year (1987)

Some of Emmitt's most amazing runs weren't much more than 10 yards. They'd get penetration into the backfield. He'd make a guy miss, shrug off another one, dart left, go right. Guys are flying around everywhere. But somehow he'd keep his balance. He'd go left, get four yards, cut right, and by the time they brought him down he had 12 yards. Nobody blocked a soul and he's got 12 yards. That's the thing that's special about him. Did he have that Bo Jackson or Deion Sanders type of speed? Absolutely not. But I think that's what made him even more special.

Jerry Odom

ERRICT RHETT

Running back (1990–93)

All-American (1993),
All-SEC (1991, '93)

He's one of the hardest working people I was ever around at the University of Florida. He had a unique trait. When we would practice running plays, he would run full speed into the end zone—every time. Normally a back will run 10 yards and come back to the huddle. I assume he wanted to think he was going to get to the end zone every time he touched the ball.

Terry Dean
on Errict Rhett

Errict was one of those guys who went full tilt. He hit the hole hard.

Danny Wuerffel

JACK YOUNGBLOOD

Defensive end (1968–70)

All-American (1970), All-SEC (1970),
Senior Bowl MOP (1971),
All-SEC Quarter Century Team (1950–74),
College Football Hall of Fame (1992),
NCAA Silver Anniversary Award (1996)

When Blood came to the Gators, he was a skinny kid. He was tall, weighed about 195 pounds. . . . Nice and easy, but very athletic. As a football player, you see strong guys, and you just never know what to make of it. Maybe a strong guy can do one thing really well. But an athletic guy can do everything, and that's what Jack was.

Steve Tannen

CHARLIE LaPRADD

Defensive tackle (1950–52)

All-American (1952), All-SEC (1952)

Charlie LaPradd was a man before the rest of us.

Doug Dickey

BRAD CULPEPPER
Defensive tackle (1988–91)
Consensus All-American (1991),
All-SEC (1991),
Draddy Trophy (nation's top scholar-athlete, 1991)

B rad Culpepper was a very, very hard worker, a disciplined type who gave it his all. Nobody had more heart than he did. People saw his work ethic and didn't think he had natural ability, but he had great natural ability. He played in the pros nine years. He's the hardest worker I have ever seen.

Kirk Kirkpatrick
tight end (1987–90)

ALEX BROWN
Defensive end (1998–2001)
All-American (1999, consensus 2001),
All-SEC (1999–2001)

F irst defensive lineman in school history to earn first team All-America honors twice. In 1999 he set school single-season QB sack record (13). Lombardi Award finalist in 2001. Completed career with school record 33 QB sacks.

2006 University of Florida
Football Guide

WILBER MARSHALL
Linebacker (1980–83)

Consensus All-American (1982, '83),
All-SEC (1981, '82, '83),
ABC National Defensive Player of the Year (1983)

You're the best linebacker I've ever seen.

John Robinson
*former Southern California head coach,
after Marshall's explosive performance
in Florida's unexpected 17–9 victory over
the Trojans in September 1982*

DAVID LITTLE
Linebacker (1977–80)

Consensus All-American (1980), All-SEC (1980)

hen David Little was a high school senior in Miami, he was the point guard for the team that won the state basketball championship. So you've got a middle linebacker who can knock your head off, but who has the athletic skills, agility, and speed to be a point guard. That's just an unbelievable combination. David was a great one. He played for the Pittsburgh Steelers for 12 years.

Tim Groves

JEVON KEARSE
Linebacker (1996–98)

All-American (1998), All-SEC (1997, '98),
Associated Press SEC Defensive Player
of the Year (1998)

J evon Kearse has been our big play guy on defense. . . . He is the guy with the ability to cause havoc with an offense.

Bob Stoops

secondary coach/defensive coordinator/assistant head coach (1996–98)

STEVE TANNEN
Defensive back (1967–69)

Consensus All-American (1969)
All-SEC (1968, '69)
SEC Defensive Back of the Year (1969)

D efensive back Steve Tannen, a first-team All-American in 1969, is tied today for sixth place for career interceptions (11). He co-holds the UF season mark for punt returns for touchdowns (2), and played in the NFL for the New York Jets (1970–1974).

Kevin M. McCarthy

FRED WEARY

Defensive back (1994–97)

Consensus All-American (1997),
All-SEC (1996, '97)

Gator cornerback Fred Weary holds the school career interception record (15).

Kevin M. McCarthy

LOUIS OLIVER

Defensive back (1985–88)

Consensus All-American (1988),
All-SEC (1987, '88)

Louis Oliver was a quiet guy, a hard worker, the enforcer on defense. You did not want to leave a receiver over the middle with him back there, because he would take his head off. His senior year he took over where Jarvis Williams left off. He was the guy who would talk in team meetings, and he was the leader.

Herbert Perry
quarterback (1987–88)

JARVIS WILLIAMS
Defensive back (1984–87)
All-American (1986, '87), All-SEC (1986, '87)

J arvis Williams was the team leader on defense, the "get-up" guy.

Herbert Perry

RAY CRISWELL
Punter (1982–85)

R ay Criswell's 44.4-yard career punting average is the best in school history.

2006 Gator Football Media Guide

JUDD DAVIS
Kicker (1992–94)
All-American (1993), All-SEC (1994), Lou Groza
Award (nation's top place-kicker, 1993)

Judd Davis made a bunch of field goals in that bad weather. Judd had a phenomenal career at Florida, and that year he won the Lou Groza award as the nation's best kicker.

Danny Wuerffel
*on the all-time Florida place-kicker,
who booted four field goals in a heavy rain
to help thwart Georgia, 33–26, in 1993*

JACQUEZ GREEN
Punt returner/kick returner (1995–97)
Consensus All-America (1997), All-SEC (1997)

Jacquez was really fast. . . . The guy could make plays. He rushed punts. He blocked some punts. He returned punts. He could do a little bit of everything. He was one of those guys, whenever he touched the ball, it could be a touchdown.

Terry Jackson

STEVE SPURRIER
Head coach (1990–2001)

National championship (1996),
six SEC championships (1991, 1993–96, 2000),
SEC Coach of the Year (1990, '91, 1994–96),
College Football Hall of Fame (1986),
Gator Football Ring of Honor (2006)

Coach Spurrier is a true player's coach. He's been on the field at Florida. He allows the players to make many of their decisions, but he expects a tremendous amount of effort, support, and productivity when it comes to playing time.

Brad Culpepper
defensive tackle (1988–91)

Clearly Steve Spurrier is one of the finest offensive coaches and strategists in all of football.

Marty Schottenheimer
former 21-year NFL head coach

He is the perfect head coach.

Shane Matthews
on Steve Spurrier

FIELDS OF PLAY

Top sportscasters everywhere call Florida Field "The Swamp." They might not really know they are saying it with a capital T as well as a capital S, but Gator fans know.

The Gainesville Sun

Fleming Field, located just north of where today's football stadium stands, hosted Gator athletic activities from 1908 through 1915, including baseball and track and field. The surface included baseball grandstands in the northwest corner of the field. Fans watched Gator action atop the hoods of their parked cars along the sidelines. [In football] the Gators were undefeated on their home field in their first 10 seasons, setting the stage for a similar home-field advantage in The Swamp, beginning in 1990.

Kevin M. McCarthy

UF football did not originate with play at Florida Field. Previously, the Gators pummeled the pigskin at old University Field, where, as one source notes, Florida lost its first home game ever (at that park) in 1916—to Alabama.

David Stirt

I t has been my hope and desire that the field be named Florida Field, after our great state, and that it be dedicated to Florida men who gave their lives in the World War. In this way no personalities are involved, and certainly we can never sufficiently perpetuate the memory of those gallant lads who gave their youth in the hope that the world might grow old in peace.

John James Tigert
UF's third university president,
1929

F lorida Field is the mecca for Gator madness and is better known by its provocative, compelling nickname—The Swamp.

David Stirt

The history of Florida Field dates back to 1930, to the dedicatory game against Alabama, on November 8. An unknown UF student named Red Barber, who would eventually turn sportscasting into an art form, handled the play-by-play. There was only one downer that festive inaugural afternoon: Florida was shut out by the Crimson Tide, 20–0.

David Stirt

I 'll never forget the feeling of running out of the tunnel at Florida Field. It gives me goose-bumps just thinking about it. I really had the time of my life out there.

Kerwin Bell
*a 1984 walk-on freshman at quarterback,
who became a two-time AP honorable-mention
All-American*

The Swamp rocked like never before, a din of noise that probably set off car alarms in the parking lot.

Pat Dooley

after the Gators' 32–29 win over
Florida State, November 23, 1997

All of those people . . . making it so loud that, standing on the 20-yard line, I finally felt what it must be like to try and call an audible in The Swamp.

Pat Dooley

The Gainesville Sun

When the Florida Gators are fuming and frolicking in their beloved Swamp, it's as if they've been dipped in magic waters. They are unbeatable.

Robbie Andreu

The feeling of playing at Florida Field is really hard to put into words. It's just an incredible sensation. When you step onto Florida Field, you are ready to play the best game of your life.

Cal Dixon
center (1988–91)

It's their players. If Florida didn't have all those great players, it would be a dry swamp.

Steve Sloan
former head coach at Vanderbilt, Texas Tech, Ole Miss, and Duke/athlete director at Alabama and Central Florida

I rank Ben Hill Griffin Stadium at Florida Field as the nation's toughest stadium. "The Swamp" is deafening.

Bob Griese
former Miami Dolphins Hall of Fame quarterback/ college football analyst

It was loud. Cover-your-ears loud. There were times it was so noisy I thought Elvis had walked into the building. But it was just Danny Wuerffel.

Pat Dooley
on the national championship celebration at Florida Field, January 11, 1997

More than anything, I'll remember all the Saturdays at Florida Field. I've played in many different stadiums, both in college and in the NFL, but nowhere is the pageantry and excitement like it is at Florida Field.

Trace Armstrong
defensive tackle (1988)

As late as 1980, Florida Field's south end zone was grandstand seating, the kind of rickety structure you'd find at high-school fields.

Peter Kerasotis

The Swamp is where Gators live. We feel comfortable there, but we hope our opponents feel tentative. A swamp is hot and sticky and can be dangerous. We feel like this is an appropriate nickname for our stadium.

Steve Spurrier

author of the now-legendary Florida Field nickname

Some great things have happened to us here over the last three years. Maybe we should start calling this place Swamp No. 2.

Steve Spurrier

on the Gator Bowl venue in Jacksonville

This is our home, our state, our stadium. We love the Gator Bowl.

Bill Gunter

defensive tackle (1989, 1991–92)

The Gator Bowl is our home away from home.

Carlton Miles

THE GREAT FLORIDA TEAMS

Florida victories are never a work of art. The Gators are more Sherwin Williams than Van Gogh. They don't outclass teams; they simply outlast them.

Mike Bianchi

on the 2006 national champion Gators

That team did what all great teams do: Someone always came through.

Tom McEwen

on the 1928 Gators, who went 8–1, losing by just a single point to Tennessee in the season finale. The '28 team led the nation in scoring and in three of their wins scored 60 or more points

That 1928 team . . . well, on a dry field, not a team in America could have beaten us.

Charley Bachman

on the one-point, 13–12, loss to Tennessee in the mud

Talk about pulling rabbits out of a hat. Why, these Gators can pull touchdowns out of a thimble.

Morgan Blake

on the 1928 Gators

Buford Long, who later played with the New York Giants, played three sports: baseball, track, and football. Rick Casares was All-SEC in football and basketball. Papa Hall had the world record in the high jump, $6'11\frac{3}{4}"$, and back then we scissored. There wasn't any Fosbury Flop. The point I'm getting at is that those guys were all two- or three-sport lettermen.

Bobby Lance

on the Florida teams of the early 1950s

T his was the best Florida season since 1928, and Coach Woodruff gets the credit for that. He recruited a lot of us.

Doug Dickey

on the 1952 Gators, the first bowl team in UF history, which edged Tulsa, 14–13, in the Gator Bowl

U p to that point our record in 1960 was the best in the history of Florida football. Our class was a pretty solid class and there were a lot of great seniors. We complemented each other pretty well. We certainly weren't a national power, but we were a good football team.

Lindy Infante

halfback (1960–62)/six-year NFL head coach with Green Bay and Indianapolis onsidering everything—the schedule, the breaks—this is the best team I've had at Florida. This is the kind of team anybody can coach. It's the kind of team capable of going the length of the field in two plays.

Ray Graves
on his 1966 Gators

e didn't know how good we REALLY were until about the fourth game, when we saw the way Tommy Durrance could run, the way John Reaves could throw, and how Carlos Alvarez could catch. Then we started thinking, "We have a DAMN good team!" We finished the season 8–1–1. It was the best record Florida ever had until that point. And we got to play Tennessee (and beat them) in the Gator Bowl.

Steve Tannen
on the 1969 Gators

I have never seen a sophomore group make so few mistakes.

Ray Graves

*on soph sensations John Reaves,
Carlos Alvarez, and Tommy Durrance,
who collaborated to crush Houston in the
1969 season opener, 59–34*

T his was the greatest effort out of the greatest bunch of players I've ever coached. Florida has never won a Southeastern Conference championship but we beat the conference champ. That should mean something. There's no question, this is the biggest win I've ever had in coaching.

Ray Graves

*after UF's 14–13 victory over Tennessee in the
1969 Gator Bowl, Graves's last game
as Florida coach*

I know now that it was the loss of (receivers) Carlos Alvarez and Andy Cheney and our offensive line that had given me so much time in 1969 that was responsible for what happened to us in 1970 and '71. It wasn't any quote by anybody. No lack of speeches and emotion. We lost players we couldn't afford to lose. But nobody wants to say that. It's too simple an answer. No drama there.

John Reaves
quarterback (1969–71), All-American 1971

With our offense, we're best at taking it the long way.

Wes Chandler
*wide receiver (1974–77),
on the 1976 and '77 Gators*

With the talent at Florida, I've thought every year that this was the year to win it. But this is a closer team than the others. Even with all the adversity and with Coach (Charley) Pell getting fired, things fell into place.

Roger Sibbald
strong safety (1980, 1982–84),
November 18, 1984

When things come easy for individuals or teams, the result doesn't mean as much. This team fought through all kinds of adversity, and that fight makes this day more special.

Kerwin Bell
on Florida's first No. 1 ranking in the 50-year
history of the Associated Press poll,
November 6, 1985

We're not unbeatable. But we're not doing too bad, are we?

Galen Hall

on the 7–0–1 start for his 1985 Gators

If I had a vote in the AP poll, I'd vote Florida No. 1, no question. This year's and last year's teams are the two best Florida teams I've seen. They have great commitment and great dedication and have justifiably been named No. 1 in America by AP.

Vince Dooley

1985

We know what we are. They can't keep me from calling myself a champion. I know what we've accomplished, and so does everybody else around the country.

Richard Fain

*cornerback (1987–90),
after the 47–15 victory over Kentucky in 1990
at Commonwealth Stadium that, were it not
for NCAA sanctions, would have given the
Gators their first-ever SEC crown*

One man doesn't make this team.

Jack Jackson

*wide receiver (1992–94),
on the '94 Gators*

God has smiled on the Gators this season.

Steve Spurrier

*after the Gators ripped Florida State
University, 52–20, in the Sugar Bowl
for the 1996 national championship*

I know one thing: Celebrating team goals with teammates is a lot better than celebrating all by yourself on some podium.

Danny Wuerffel

after the 1997 Sugar Bowl win over Florida State for the national championship

Everyone said, "This offense ain't gonna work. This ain't Utah. There's too much speed [in the SEC]." Well, look where we are now.

Andre Caldwell

on the 2006 Gators and coach Urban Meyer's spread-option offense, prior to the BCS National Championship Game matchup with Ohio State. Meyer brought the high-octane offense with him from the University of Utah

We proved that the SEC is the best conference in America. We shut everybody up.

Steven Harris

on the 2006 Gators

We expect these guys to be right back in this position next year. That's what you expect out of the Gator team every season, to compete for an SEC and national title.

Chris Leak
on the 2007 Gators

What's the future look like? I think it looks really good. That's part of the reason why our staff went to Florida, because you can recruit the best players in the country at that place.

Urban Meyer
2007

It is Tim Tebow's team as of right now. It is Tim Tebow's team and a lot of these young players will have to pick up the slack.

Urban Meyer
on the 2007 Gators

THE GREAT RIVALRIES

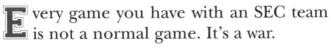

Every game you have with an SEC team is not a normal game. It's a war.

Shane Matthews

The Rivals

It is the chief ingredient spicing up the tantalizing recipe of college football—rivalries.

Much has been written about "The World's Largest Outdoor Cocktail Party"—the annual altercation between Florida and Georgia. The vaunted series with Auburn began way back in 1911. And of course, there's that tempestuous instate shootout with those pesky neighbors from Tallahassee that didn't get off the ground until 1958.

For many Gator fans, it's the annual showdown with Tennessee that defines UF's SEC season. Those who think the series began with Peyton Manning's futile attempts to down Florida in the mid-1990s have some history to learn. It was back in 1928 that this series initiated its venom, when the Vols ended what would have been a Rose Bowl season for an undefeated Gators team, with a slim one-point victory in the mud at Knoxville.

An unusual situation was brought to the 1969 Gator Bowl meeting between the two schools, when UT head coach Doug Dickey was rumored to be leaving Knoxville for, of all places, Gainesville. One of UF's sweetest victories ever was the 14–13 win engineered by coach Ray Graves in his last game for the Gators, over those Dickey-led Vols.

My players were soaked to the skin. We had on those old ribbed stockings. They were carrying a couple of pounds of mud each. I had my boys take off their stockings. We were lighter without them. I waited until the last minute to take the team back out into the rain. Alabama was already lined up for the kickoff, and later Coach (Wallace) Wade would be furious. He said we left them standing there to get wet and cold while we delayed. He was so mad he never spoke to me again. But, as I remember, he had his boys play barelegged in the future in bad weather.

Maj. James A. Van Fleet
*on UF's 16–6 win in Birmingham,
November 29, 1923*

The haunting 13–12 loss to Tennessee in 1928

It is legend now.

It may well rank as the toughest defeat in Florida football history: the one-point loss to Tennessee in the 1928 season finale, 13–12, on the cold, muddy slush of Shields-Watkins Field in Knoxville.

Going into the game the Gators, Rose Bowl-bound with a win, were undefeated and led the nation in scoring behind a volatile backfield that included the ambidextrous Clyde "Cannonball" Crabtree, future Chicago Bears star Carl Brumbaugh, and Red Bethea. Also figuring prominently in Florida's fortunes throughout the season was the school's first-ever first-team All-American, end Dale Van Sickel.

Tennessee also roared into the game undefeated, with only a scoreless tie with Kentucky the week before to tarnish its record. The Vols were riding the bright glare of "The Flaming Sophomores"—quarterback Bobby Dodd, All-America halfback Gene McEver and running back Buddy Hackman—to victory after victory that season. Only once in three years would the trio know defeat.

Tennessee scored first, with McEver plunging over and Dodd hitting E. H. Alley for the one-point conversion. Florida scored next on the running of Crabtree and Brumbaugh and Crabtree's passing. However, Brumbaugh's crucial pass attempt for the point after failed. But the play that turned the game around was an attempted lateral from Crabtree to Brumbaugh.

"He was open," opined a still-disappointed Crabtree years later. "If I'd pulled it off, we'd have had a score."

On the play, the Florida quarterback's arm was hit by the Vols' Dave McArthur just as Crabtree released the ball. Tennessee's Hackman intercepted the pitch and dashed 70 yards for the go-ahead score. Dodd failed to kick the extra point, and it stood 13–6 in favor of Tennessee.

After a Florida drive stalled at the UT 2, Dodd, one of the nation's all-time brilliant punters, mishit a Tennessee punt, and the Gators took over at the Volunteer 30-yard line.

Florida came back strong on a 29-yard pass from Brumbaugh to Tommy Owens that went down to the 1, from where Crabtree took it in. It looked like a tie was inevitable—a fitting, albeit disappointing, ending to the titanic battle. But it all unraveled as Brumbaugh's point-after kick was blocked.

The heartbreaking 13–12 final score would haunt the 1928 Gator team members for the rest of their lives.

I felt awful at the time, but I feel worse every year that passes. I never knew it would mean so much to us all.

Clyde "Cannonball" Crabtree
on the immortal one-point, 13–12, season-ending loss to Tennessee in 1928 that wiped out the Gators' undefeated campaign and Rose Bowl hopes

Neither Gen. Neyland's being in a wheelchair nor the wet ground caused us to miss the two points or not to complete that lateral to Brumbaugh, I can see it now. I have seen it for nearly half a century.

Charley Bachman
on the 13–12 loss to Tennessee in 1928

T hat No. 74 was pretty tough. He was slugging a time or two.

Bobby Scott

*former Tennessee quarterback,
on UF defensive end Jack Youngblood, after
the 1969 Gator Bowl, won by Florida, 14–13*

I t's a lot more satisfying to beat the Southeastern Conference champion than the Lambert Trophy winner.

Ray Graves

*after defeating Tennessee in the 1969
Gator Bowl. Under Graves, Florida had
beaten Penn State in the 1962
Gator Bowl, 17–7*

This was the biggest game in Tennessee history, but the Vols came out looking like a bunch of opossums in the headlights of an 18-wheeler. By the time they began to play like it was just a game, Florida was up 35–0.

Pat Dooley
*on the start of the 1996 UT-UF game
in Knoxville, won by Florida, 35–29*

Given the programs' pedigrees and their assignments to the same division, the winner on the third Saturday of September becomes the favorite to win the East. The loser, meanwhile, has rallied to take the division twice in 15 years.

Dave Curtis
on Florida-Tennessee through the 2006 season

I f you are ever going back to Albany, Ga., you'd better put it through there.

Ray Graves

to Wayne Barfield, before the kicker's 31-yard field goal against Georgia with 29 seconds left at Jacksonville, November 12, 1967, gave Florida a 17–16 win over the Bulldogs

G eorgia-Florida is a wild series in which the unexpected has become the expected, in which high drama has become routine. There's only one safe prediction that can be made about the game Saturday. It won't be 75–0.

Bob Bassine

The Florida Times-Union, November 9, 1968. Bassine's outlandish prediction wasn't far off the mark. Georgia blasted Florida, 51–0

The game boiled down to the fact that Florida is a better football team. Coming in we thought they had a great team. Unfortunately we were right.

Pat Dye

former Auburn head coach,
on UF's 14–10 defeat of the Tigers in 1985

This was Florida-Auburn, No. 2 vs. No. 6, bloodbath, shootout, heated rivalry, and all that. The kind of game you don't leave unless a bone is showing.

Larry Guest

Orlando Sentinel, *November 3, 1985,*
on Auburn running back Bo Jackson's
controversial self-removal from the game for
what some observers felt was a minor injury
(thigh/knee). Upon gaining 48 first-half yards,
Jackson retired after only four carries in the
second half. Florida toppled the Tigers, 14–10

D uring the Spurrier era, the Gators went 11–1 against Georgia and 9–3 against Auburn, for a combined 20–4 mark. By the time he left, it was Georgia that was talking about moving the game out of Jacksonville. The mindset had done a 180, for both schools.

Peter Kerasotis

> **FAST FACT:** *Prior to Spurrier's arrival in Gainesville, talk around UF often centered on vying for a switch of the annual Georgia-Florida game from Jacksonville to the standard home/away series, alternating between Athens and Gainesville, such was Georgia's domination of the Gators in Jacksonville.*

T oday's inaugural meeting between the University of Florida's Fighting Gators and Florida State University's Seminoles is without a doubt the most talked about game in the State's history.

Jimmy Gay
UF director of sports publicity, 1958

Strong-armed bandits dressed in University of Florida football suits and guilty of malice aforethought, made a nightmare out of brash Florida State U's fondest dream Saturday, crushing the Seminoles 21–7 before 43,000 fans.

Jim Minter

Atlanta Journal-Constitution,
November 23, 1958

I have no friends at FSU. Seems to me that they get all the Florida rejects.

Tom Shannon

Once the Gators got cooking, the Seminoles were little more than tattered hemophiliacs . . . the bleeding just wouldn't stop.

Hubert Mizell

St. Petersburg Times, *December 4, 1983,*
after Florida vaporized Florida State, 53–14

It was one of the most emotional games I've been around as a player or a coach. The electricity—it was like every play, the game depended on it.

Steve Spurrier

on the 14–9 victory over Florida State in 1991, decided by the Gators' late fourth-quarter defensive stand. The win assured Florida of a Sugar Bowl berth and its first 10-win season in school annals

When I was in college and we played Florida State, you definitely wanted to beat them, because you would say, "God, we can't lose to Florida State. It was only 20 years ago when they were a girls' school."

Steve Tannen

I t started right there, when they started dancing on our field. This is our field, our house and they weren't going to take it. The fight started then and it just went on from there. We got hyped up. You can't dance on our field.

Jevon Kearse
outside linebacker (1996–98),
on pregame boogie antics by several
Seminole players on the giant "F" at Florida
Field in 1997. The Gators rushed to midfield,
pushing, shoving, and shouting at the FSU
players. Florida utilized the incident as an
emotional springboard to vault past
No. 2-ranked Florida State, 32–29

That's huge for us to beat all three of our big rivals for the second year in a row. If you're a Gator, you get judged on how you do against Tennessee, Georgia and, of course, Florida State.

Tim Tebow

on the 2005–06 sweep of the Gators'
big rivals

Not even the most delusional Gators fan could have envisioned a scenario where UF would win the national title the same year FSU and Miami played in second-rate bowls. FSU in the Emerald Bowl? Miami in the MPC Computers Bowl? C'monnnnn. Some Florida fan must have a lamp, a genie, and a Ouija board.

Jemele Hill

"Page 2" columnist/ESPN the Magazine writer,
on the 2006 national champions and
UF's two in-state rivals

If you can't get up for Florida State, then you're not breathing.

Don Gaffney

WINNING
AND LOSING

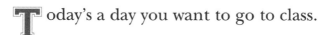

Today's a day you want to go to class.

Leon Pennington
linebacker (1982–85),
on the feeling of being ranked No. 1 for the
first time in school history, November 6, 1985

All stood shoulder to shoulder and responded with the best they had. While victory never smiled on them, they have the admiration and satisfaction of a loyal student body (about 300 boys at the time) that supported them through all the trials and troubles of defeat.

1916 Seminole
University of Florida yearbook,
on the winless, 0–5 Gators of 1916, who
scored a mere three points the entire season
and were shut out in four games

Next to my pledge to try to get the cows outlawed from public highways (which he achieved), my pledge to try to get that winning team at Florida seemed to get the most applause.

Fuller Warren
former governor of Florida,
1948

I 've often been asked, "What's the dif-ference between winning and losing?" Let me give you an example. In 1950 we beat Vanderbilt. When the fans came out to meet us at the airfield, they took us back to campus in convertibles. Two games later we went to Kentucky and got clobbered. This time, when we flew back to Gainesville, they picked us up in some old yellow school busses, and we had two flat tires. It took us two hours to get from the airfield to downtown. Nobody came out. There wasn't anything but tumble-weeds out across the field.

Red Mitchum
offensive tackle (1950–51)

To win the Heisman Trophy without being on national TV is like winning the presidential election without winning California. Without Norm Carlson, Steve Spurrier doesn't win the Heisman Trophy. Spurrier should at least give one of the arms to Norm.

Beano Cook

*longtime college football analyst,
on the behind-the-scenes efforts of Florida's
former sports information director to secure
the 1966 Heisman Trophy for Spurrier*

After the stunning victory, Charley Pell ran around Florida Field that shook with a deafening roar, high-fiving giddy fans with such pure unadulterated joy that the image is still indelibly imprinted on the personal memories of those who witnessed the scene.

Peter Kerasotis

*on the Gators' stunning 17–9 upset of
Southern California in 1982*

Blame the team. He has no eligibility. It's not his fault if he shows us, tells us, and we don't do it. It's no more fun for us to lose than for those in the stands.

Glenn Cameron

linebacker (1972–74),
defending his coach under siege, Doug Dickey,
when the Gators stood 2–4 after dropping
four straight games in 1973

I don't remember Coach Dickey fumbling all year.

Lee McGriff

wide receiver (1972–74),
UF ended the four-game losing streak in 1973
with the upset of Auburn at Jordan-Hare
Stadium, considered one of the biggest wins
in school history

Of all the victories I've ever been associated with, this ranks right at the top. This is the one we needed.

Doug Dickey

*at the conclusion of Florida's 12–8 upset
of Auburn at Jordan-Hare Stadium in 1973,
after the Gators had lost four straight*

A great win means there's a chance for a greater one ahead.

Doug Dickey

It was way back in 1982 when I first went to Neyland Stadium as an assistant at Duke and in 1988 and 1989 as a head coach. The winner of the Florida-Tennessee game has a huge advantage in the Eastern Division and a huge advantage trying to get to the conference championship game. It doesn't always work out that way, but the winner is in excellent shape.

Steve Spurrier

When you're No. 1 you walk a little lighter on your feet.

Scott Armstrong
inside linebacker (1984–86)

I remember what coach Bill Alexander used to say at Georgia Tech: It's better to just beat 'em and let 'em try to figure all year the many ways they could have won.

Ray Graves

We came back to beat a team that has a great tradition and we did it in their backyard. You have to have something special inside you to do that.

Glenn Neely
*offensive tackle (1987–90),
on Florida's 17–13 upset win over Alabama
in 1990, in which UF intercepted a pass
on its own 2-yard line, completed a 70-yard
bomb from the end zone, and blocked a
fourth-quarter punt*

Once a coach or a player gets used to losing, and it doesn't hurt them anymore, then they're going to be losers. But while you try to win, you play by the rules. It's not worth it if you won in any way illegally.

Steve Spurrier

I remember our first team meeting when Coach Spurrier got here. He was telling us we were going to win, that we were going to be champions. It was just an attitude, and he made you believe.

Jerry Odom

There's some principles and guidelines that winners have, and I just tried to instill those in the team. Fortunately, all the guys bought into it.

Steve Spurrier

We were about to get the razor blades out. If we had blown that game, it would've been the worst choke in history.

Brad Culpepper

on the Gators' 35–26 win over Kentucky in 1991. Florida led at one time, 28–6, before allowing Kentucky to close within two points, 28–26. The win gave UF its first official SEC title

We were in control. No, make that we thought we were in control.

Shane Matthews

quarterback (1990–92), on the 1991 Kentucky game that almost slipped from the Gators' grasp

We won the close one. There were people doubting us in the close ones before today. Now we can say we can play 60 minutes and win a close one.

Larry Kennedy
on the 24–23 thriller over Alabama in the 1994 SEC title game

I wouldn't want to win any other way than the way we did tonight. A blowout wouldn't have meant as much as this does.

Kevin Carter
on UF's one-point win over the Crimson Tide in the 1994 SEC championship game

All that was left after the first quarter was to pencil in the final score, as the Gators emptied another stadium prematurely.

Pat Dooley

on Florida's 52–17 rout of Georgia at Sanford Stadium, October 28, 1995—the first UF-UGA game in Athens since 1932

I don't care about the numbers. All I care about are the letters, and we got the W.

James Bates

linebacker (1993–96), on being outgained by Tennessee by nearly 200 yards and giving up almost 500 yards passing to the Vols' Peyton Manning. Yet on September 21, 1996, Florida exited Knoxville with a 35–29 win

If one of those NFL teams wants to win a Super Bowl, they ought to get Danny Wuerffel. He won the state championship, now the national championship. Logically, he could win a Super Bowl for anybody.

Steve Spurrier

All the awards and travel have been nice, and they'll be great memories. But the greatest memories are winning and hugging your teammates after big wins.

Danny Wuerffel

It wasn't just that Spurrier won football games; he won with a swagger. And he won big.

Peter Kerasotis

Winning's all that matters.

Urban Meyer

GATOR BITES

We've kind of turned Ohio State into Runner-up U., haven't we?

Steve Spurrier

April 2007,
after UF's back-to-back victories over
the Buckeyes in both the 2006 football and
basketball national championship games

H e-e-e-e-e-r-r-r-r-r-r-r-e come the Gators!

Jim Finch
longtime Florida Field public address announcer

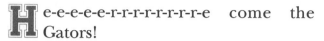

W itt Palmer (alumni president) sent me a medal that was blessed by the Pope in Rome. He said if I'd keep it in my pocket, we'd beat Auburn, and we sure did. I'm not Catholic, but I may have to go to Mass after this.

Doug Dickey
after his Gators upset Auburn, 12–8, at Jordan-Hare Stadium in 1973, after losing their four previous games

A ll Gators want something that says "national" on it.

Steve Spurrier

No. 22 a Family Affair

It began with the revolutionary presence of the first black man to play football for the University of Florida, in 1970, and continued through 1998 with the appearance of that man's second son on the Gainesville campus. It was a line of family succession that bred a UF novelty: all wore Gator jersey number 22.

Pioneering UF wide receiver Willie Jackson Sr. first wore the double-deuce digits during his standout career in Gainesville, from 1970 through '73. Next came Willie's son, Willie Jackson Jr., a premier Gator wideout from 1990 through '93 who later played for the Chicago Bears. Finally, running back Terry Jackson, who starred for the Gators most recently, from 1995 through '98, donned the special number.

"The tradition goes on," said Willie Jackson Sr. in the fall of 1995, "It was exciting to know you were the first to do it, then see your oldest son do it, and now your youngest son doing it. It's wonderful."

It didn't hurt that a couple of other UF gems, John L. Williams and Emmitt Smith among others, added some luster to the jersey number along the way.

My freshman year Gatorade had already been invented. In fact, when we had our first water break, they gave us Gatorade, which I had never had before. It was the original potion, which wasn't sweet. But it was 120 degrees, and it sure tasted good.

John Reaves

Dr. Cade began experimenting with Gatorade my freshman year. He tried to kill us all! That first stuff was lethal! It was thick, like syrup, and had an aftertaste. Then it started to look like milk. It was all brand new to us. We'd never had anything like that. Water with salt in it was the closest thing we ever had.

Jack Youngblood

When we come out of the huddle, let's holler something at 'em even if we have to take it back.

Curtis King

tackle (1950–52),
upon sizing up teammate Red Mitchum's
condition in the UF huddle in a game against
Kentucky in the early 1950s. Mitchum had
been pitted against Wildcat All-America
tackle Bob Gain, who had broken Mitchum's
nose, chipped his cheekbone, and knocked out
a molar during the course of play

Nobody can have hair longer than mine.

Galen Hall

facetiously telling a player about his rules
on length of hair. Hall is bald

Gators beget Gators beget ...

Three University of Florida quarterbacks—Steve Spurrier (1966), John Reaves (1971), and Kerwin Bell (1987)—all concluded their collegiate careers as the SEC's all-time leader passer.

Smithsonian

When future NFL Hall of Famer Emmitt Smith was a freshman at Florida, in 1987, he became the fastest freshman in college football history to reach 1,000 yards rushing, achieving the feat in his seventh game.

Two No. 1s

In the 1986 NFL draft, fullback John L. Williams (Seattle) and running back Neal Anderson (Chicago) were both picked in the first round, the first time two running backs from the same school had been selected in the opening round since 1971.

This system is so much fun to play. It is fun to have the challenge of playing man-to-man and bump-and-run all over the field. If you are a true competitor, this is the type of scheme you love to play and it showcases your skills.

Fred Weary
defensive back (1994–97)

Let's do it in football now!

Joakim Noah
*Gators basketball star,
after Florida won the 2006
NCAA Men's Basketball Tournament*

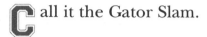all it the Gator Slam.

Associated Press

*after Florida's victory over Ohio State in the
2006 BCS National Championship Game
established the Gators as the first team in
college history to hold both the national
football and basketball crowns in the same
year. Florida's hoopsters then repeated as
national champs in 2007, ironically taking
down Ohio State in the NCAA Championship
Game, positioning UF as the only college ever
to hold both titles in the same school year*

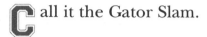ne chomp, two champs.

Mike Bianchi

*on Florida's dual football/basketball
collegiate champions of 2006*

FLORIDA NATIONAL CHAMPION ROSTERS

While it took the Gators 90 years to win their first national championship, the SEC power, in 2006, made up for lost time with its second crown in 10 years. Beyond the galaxy of dazzling stars that have always sparkled in the Florida gridiron expanse, the everyday unsung contributors have been many. UF's twin championship laurels could not have happened without the chomp of the following Gator players.

1996

12–1

(includes 52–20 Sugar Bowl victory over Florida State)
Steve Spurrier, *head coach*

	Pos	Ht	Wt	Yr	Hometown
Allen, Tremayne	TE	6–2	234	Sr	Knoxville, TN
Anthony, Reidel	WR	6–0	181	Jr	South Bay
Badeaux Ernie	DT	6–4	273	Fr	River Ridge
Baker, Tyrone	WR	5–9	168	Jr	Gainesville
Bates, James	LB	6–1	234	Sr	Sevierville, TN
Battle, Ronnie	CB	5–8	170	Jr	Ft. Myers
Beauchamp, Tim	DE	6–2	255	So	New Smyrna Beach
Blackshear, Cheston	G	6–3	272	Fr	Jacksonville
Brindise, Noah	QB	6–3	232	Jr	Ft. Myers
Brown, Teako	FS	5–11	190	So	Miami
Browning, Pat	G	6–4	294	So	Tampa
Bryan, Scott	OT	6–4	273	Fr	Longwood
Buchanan, Zuri	LB	6–0	222	Fr	DeSoto, Texas
Bullard, Thaddeus	DE	6–3	236	Fr	Live Oak
Campbell, Jayme	FB	6–2	247	Fr	Alachua
Carlisle, Cooper	OT	6–5	285	Fr	McComb, MS
Carroll, Daymon	RB	5–9	160	Fr	Norristown, PA
Chambers, Derrick	DE	6–4	267	Fr	Lawndale, NC
Chester, Ed	DT	6–4	274	So	Spring Hill
Cohens, Willie	DE	6–3	255	So	Starke
Collins, Mo	OT	6–5	312	So	Charlotte, NC
Council, Keith	DT	6–5	273	Jr	Orlando
Davis, Cameron	DE	6–4	255	Sr	Lauderhill
Davis, Reggie	FS	6–0	178	Fr	Bradenton
Dean, Jason	WR	5–10	177	Sr	Naples
Dubose, Ernie	FB	5–10	201	Jr	Port Charlotte
Dudley, Craig	WR	5–8	177	Fr	Ft. Lauderdale
Edge, Dwight	TE	6–6	220	Fr	Apopka
Edmiston, Bart	PK	5–10	169	Sr	Pensacola
Evans, Jerome	FB	6–1	240	Sr	Arcadia
Ferguson, McDonald	DT	6–1	252	Sr	Miami
Frazier, Rod	FB	5–11	213	Fr	Bradenton
George, Tony	SS	5–11	187	So	Cincinnati, Ohio
Graddy, Rod	FS	6–1	194	Fr	Cuthbert, GA
Green, Jacquez	WR	5–9	163	So	Ft. Valley, GA
Gurley, Buck	DE	6–2	262	Fr	Tallahassee
Hagberg, Fred	LS	6–1	241	Jr	Hialeah
Harris, Mike	FS	6–1	195	Jr	Gainesville
Hilliard, Ike	WR	6–0	184	Jr	Patterson, LA

All hometowns are in Florida unless otherwise noted.

Holland, Todd	OT	6–6	274	Jr	Orlando
Jackson, Demetric	SS	6–0	175	Sr	Ft. White
Jackson, Terry	TB/LB	6–0	213	So	Gainesville
Johnson, Doug	QB	6–2	195	Fr	Gainesville
Kalich, Ryan	G	6–3	282	Fr	Houston, Texas
Karim, Nafis	WR	5–11	174	So	Marietta, GA
Kearse, Jevon	LB	6–5	239	Fr	Ft. Myers
Kelsey, Keith	LB	6–0	218	Fr	Newberry
Kinney, Erron	TE	6–6	256	Fr	Ashland, VA
Ladd, Sean	OT	6–4	265	So	Potomac, MD
Lewis, Demetrius	DB	6–0	198	Fr	Decatur, GA
Lott, Anthone	CB	5–9	193	Sr	Jacksonville
McCaslin, Eugene	TB	6–1	203	Fr	Tampa
McCray, Xavier	LB	5–11	212	Jr	Miami
McGrew, Reggie	DT	6–2	281	Fr	Mayo
McGriff, Travis	WR	5–8	177	So	Gainesville
Mitchell, Anthony	DE	6–5	251	Fr	Louisville, MS
Mitchell, Jeff	C	6–5	291	Sr	Clearwater
Mobley, Dwayne	FB	5–10	231	Sr	Brooksville
Moten, Mike	DT	6–5	266	Jr	Daytona Beach
Nabavi, David	WR	5–10	191	Sr	Orlando
Nunn, Shawn	TE	6–3	259	Sr	Ocala
Owens, Daryl	LB	5–10	213	Fr	Jackson, MS
Peterson, Mike	LB	6–1	210	So	Alachua
Piller, Zach	OT	6–5	306	So	Tallahassee
Pollard, Dock	CB	5–8	173	Fr	Bradenton
Richardson, Jamie	WR	5–11	178	Fr	Tallahassee
Ritch, Wyley	C	6–4	272	Jr	Ft. White
Rodgers, Willie	DE	6–1	246	Jr	Miami
Ross, Taras	TE	6–2	233	Jr	Dade City
Rutledge, Johnny	LB	6–2	229	Sr	Belle Glade
Schottenheimer, Brian	QB	6–2	198	Sr	Overland Park, KS
Showers, Shea	CB	5–11	171	Sr	Alachua
Sims, Teddy	LB	6–0	222	Fr	Belle Glade
Skinner, Ian	WR	5–7	162	Fr	Miami
Stevenson, Robby	P	6–1	190	So	Bradenton
Story, Deac	G	6–4	281	So	Winter Park
Taylor, Fred	TB	6–1	222	Jr	Belle Glade
Teague, Matt	PK/P	6–1	176	Sr	Keystone Heights
Thomas, Dwayne	LB	6–3	229	Jr	Jacksonville
Walton, Kavin	LB	6–0	214	Jr	Miami
Warren, Cedric	CB	5–9	168	Fr	Virginia Beach, VA
Weary, Fred	CB	5–10	180	Jr	Jacksonville
Williams, Elijah	TB	5–10	185	Jr	Milton
Wright, Lawrence	SS	6–1	212	Sr	Miami
Wuerffel, Danny	QB	6–2	209	Sr	Ft. Walton Beach
Xynidis, Jon	SS	5–10	190	Jr	Daytona Beach
Yarbrough, Corey	C	6–2	285	Fr	Glen St. Mary
Young, Donnie	G	6–4	315	Sr	Venice
Zedalis, Zac	G	6–3	279	Fr	Alachua

2006

13–1
(includes 41–14 BCS National Championship Game
victory over Ohio State)
Urban Meyer, *head coach*

	Pos	Ht	Wt	Yr	Hometown
Alford, Lutrell	DL	6–2	292	Jr	Gainesville
Anderson, Markihe	CB	5–9	175	Fr	Fort Myers
Antwine, Brandon	DT	6–0	278	Fr	Garland, TX
Baker, Dallas	WR	6–3	207	Rsr	New Smyrna Beach
Baldry, Derek	TE	6–4	262	Rso	Gainesville
Barrie, Jim	OL	6–5	282	Fr	Tampa
Bennett, Alex	ATH	6–1	193	Fr	Atlanta, GA
Bentley, Lumar	DB	6–0	155	Rsr	Ft. Myers
Blackett, Roderick	LB	5–8	217	Rfr	Pompano Beach
Blaylock, Andrew	QB	6–1	190	Fr	Durham, NC
Boateng, Nyan	WR	6–1	204	So	Brooklyn, NY
Brewer, Cam	WR	5–9	174	So	Gainesville
Brooks, Nick	CB	6–0	206	Rsr	Warner Robins, GA
Caldwell, Andre	WR	6–1	203	Rjr	Tampa
Campbell, Lorenzo	DB	5–11	205	Rso	Coral Springs
Carodine, Miguel	DB	6–0	187	Fr	Gainesville
Carr, Curtis	S	5–10	175	So	Gainesville
Casey, Tate	TE	6–7	240	Jr	Longview, TX
Codrington, Simon	OL	6–6	300	Rfr	Miami
Cohen, Joe	DT	6–2	296	Sr	Melbourne
Concepcion, Telly	DB	5–6	153	Rso	Tampa
Cooper, Riley	WR	6–3	206	Fr	Clearwater
Cornelius, Jemalle	WR	5–11	185	Rsr	Fort Meade
Crum, Brian	LB	6–3	235	Rsr	Woodbine, GA
Cunningham, Jermaine	DE	6–4	225	Fr	Stone Mountain, GA
Curtis, John	S	6–2	205	Rso	Rockledge
Demps, Jon	LB	6–4	230	So	Pensacola
Deveaux, Jamaal	LB	6–0	227	Rfr	Port St. Lucie
Doe, Dustin	LB	6–0	215	Fr	Jasper
Estopinan, Javier	DL	6–2	278	Rso	Miami
Everett, Earl	LB	6–3	234	Sr	Webster
Fairbanks, John	DL	6–4	260	Fr	Celebration
Fayson, Jarred	WR	6–0	200	Fr	Tampa

Fritze, Andrew	K	6–0	186	Rfr	Ponce Inlet
Gilbert, Marcus	OL	6–6	298	Fr	Fort Lauderdale
Gresham, Darryl Jr.	DE	6–3	255	Rfr	Roanoke, VA
Guandolo, Mark	QB	5–8	168	Fr	Hollywood
Guilford, Michael	QB	6–0	181	Fr	Quincy
Harrell, Alex	P	5–9	170	Fr	Boca Raton
Harris, Steven	DT	6–5	285	Rsr	Miami
Harvey, Derrick	DE	6–5	262	Rso	Greenbelt, MD
Harvin, Percy	WR	5–11	180	Fr	Virginia Beach, VA
Haupt, Eddie	OL	6–4	295	Rfr	Merritt Island
Hetland, Chris	K	6–0	186	Rsr	Leesburg, GA
Hiers, Brad	OL	6–6	285	Rfr	Bartow
Higgins, Tim	WR	5–7	172	Sr	Northville, MI
Hobbs, Corey	OL	6–3	320	Fr	Oviedo
Holliday, Cade	WR	5–11	186	Rfr	Gainesville
Hornsby, Jamar	S	6–2	192	Fr	Jacksonville
Howard, Bo	FB	5–10	221	Fr	Ponte Vedra Beach
Hurt, Maurice	OL	6–3	309	Fr	Milledgeville, GA
Ijjas, Joey	K	6–2	204	Rjr	Clearwater
Ingram, Cornelius	TE	6–4	225	Rso	Hawthorne
Jackson, Kyle	S	6–1	200	Jr	Neptune Beach
James, Brandon	RB	5–7	180	Fr	St. Augustine
Johnson, Andrew	FB	6–0	237	Rfr	Parkland
Johnson, Carl	OL	6–5	328	Fr	Durham, NC
Joiner, Tony	S	6–0	208	Jr	Haines City
Jones, A. J.	LB	6–2	200	Fr	Tampa
Kane, Bobby	K	6–0	187	Rfr	Coconut Creek
Kendrick, Brandon	RB	6–0	179	Rfr	Gainesville
Latsko, Billy	HB	5–10	232	Rsr	Gainesville
Leak, Chris	QB	6–0	207	Sr	Charlotte, NC
Lewis, Reggie	CB	5–10	196	Rsr	Jacksonville
Manson, Markus	RB	6–0	210	Rso	Tuscaloosa, AL
Marsh, Lawrence	DE	6–5	275	Fr	Augusta, GA
McCollum, Jermaine	CB	5–9	185	Rsr	Miami
McCollum, Tremaine	CB	5–8	175	Rsr	Miami
McDonald, Ray	DE	6–3	280	Rsr	Belle Glade
McMillan, Clint	DT	6–1	285	Rjr	Oviedo
Medder, Carlton	OL	6–5	315	Rjr	Clermont
Miller, Drew	OL	6–5	305	Jr	Sarasota
Moore, Kestahn	RB	5–10	212	So	Arlington, Texas
Moss, Jarvis	DE	6–6	251	Rjr	Denton, Texas
Munroe, Dorian	S	5–11	200	Rfr	Miami

Murphy, Louis	WR	6–2	197	So	St. Petersburg
Nappy, Eric	K	5–11	182	Rsr	Gainesville
Nelson, David	WR	6–5	206	Rfr	Wichita Falls, TX
Nelson, Reggie	DB	6–1	193	Jr	Melbourne
Newell, Kyle	OL	6–8	284	Rfr	Tampa
Paul, Moise	CB	6–0	221	Rjr	Brooklyn, NY
Phillips, Jonathan	K	5–10	197	So	Wellington
Pierre-Louis, Wondy	CB	6–1	185	Fr	Naples
Pintado, Chris	LB	6–1	214	Fr	Miami
Pupello, Kyle	FB	6–0	238	Rjr	Tampa
Pupello, Trent	TE	6–2	251	Fr	Tampa
Rickerson, Jacques	CB	5–10	176	Fr	St. Augustine
Rissler, Steve	OL	6–3	306	Sr	Sarasota
Robinson, Darryon	LB	6–0	226	Sr	Gainesville
Rowley, Butch	LS/QB	6–1	200	Rso	Orlando
Rutledge, Eric	HB	6–0	245	Jr	Gainesville
Sanders, Terron	DT	6–1	315	Fr	Bradenton
Shelton, Vernon	DL	6–0	255	Rso	Gainesville
Sheppard, Lamont	CB	5–9	180	Rso	Jacksonville
Siler, Brandon	LB	6–2	235	Jr	Orlando
Sledge, Eric	LB	6–2	210	Rfr	Apopka
Smith, James	LS	6–1	233	Rso	Gainesville
Smith, Ryan	CB	5–10	165	Jr	Diamond Bar, CA
Sorrentino, Joey	WR	5–7	174	Rfr	Ocala
Spikes, Brandon	LB	6–3	240	Fr	Shelby, NC
Stamper, Ryan	LB	6–2	226	Rfr	Jacksonville
Tartt, Jim	OL	6–3	315	Rso	Sopchoppy
Taussig, Greg	K	6–0	194	So	Winter Park
Tebow, Tim	QB	6–3	229	Fr	Jacksonville
Thomas, Bryan	S	6–2	193	Fr	Zephyrhills
Thomas, Marcus	DT	6–3	296	Sr	Jacksonville
Tookes, Kenneth	WR	6–2	207	Rsr	Jacksonville
Trautwein, Phil	OL	6–6	308	Jr	Voorhees, NJ
Walker, Chevon	RB	5–10	195	Fr	Fort Myers
Watkins, Jason	OL	6–6	307	Rso	Lakeland
Wilbur, Eric	P	6–2	200	Sr	Winter Park
Williams, Justin	WR	6–1	195	Fr	Folkston, GA
Williams, Mon	RB	6–2	195	Fr	Mesquite, TX
Williamson, Mike	LS	5–11	195	Rfr	Winter Park
Wilson, Ronnie	OL	6–3	312	Rfr	Pompano Beach
Worton, Cody	S	6–1	185	Fr	Homestead
Wynn, DeShawn	RB	5–11	238	Rsr	Cincinnati, OH

BIBLIOGRAPHY

Biddle, Joe. "Florida's Swamp Hazardous to Foes' Health." *The Tennessean.* 12 Sept. 1999: 4C.

Cobb, Arthur. *Go Gators!* Pensacola, Fla.: Sunshine Publishing Co., 1967.

Conley, Cale. *Sunshine Hate.* Atlanta, Ga.: Gridiron Publishers, 1993.

———. *War Between the States.* Atlanta, Ga.: Gridiron Publishers, 1992.

Gay, Jimmy, ed. 1956 University of Florida Brochure. Gainesville, Fla.: University of Florida Athletic Association, 1956.

Golenbock, Peter. *Go Gators! An Oral History of Florida's Pursuit of Gridiron Glory.* St. Petersburg, Fla.: Legends Publishing, 2002.

Humenik, John, ed. *1986 Florida Football Guide.* Gainesville, Fla.: University of Florida Athletic Association, 1986.

———. *1987 Florida Football Guide.* Gainesville, Fla.: University of Florida Athletic Association, 1987.

———. *1992 University of Florida Football Guide.* Gainesville, Fla.: University of Florida Athletic Association, 1992.

———. *1996 University of Florida Football Guide.* Gainesville, Fla.: University of Florida Athletic Association, 1996.

———. *1998 University of Florida Football Guide.* Gainesville, Fla.: University of Florida Athletic Association, 1998.

Jones, James P. and Kevin M. McCarthy. *The Gators and the Seminoles: Honor, Guts and Glory.* Gainesville, Fla.: Maupin House, 1993.

Kerasotis, Peter. *Stadium Stories: Florida Gators.* Guilford, Conn.: The Globe Pequot Press, 2005.

Martin, W. F. Buddy. *Down Where the Old Gators Play.* Dubuque, Iowa: Kendall/Hunt Publishing Co., 1995.

McCarthy, Kevin M. *Fightin' Gators: A History of University of Florida Football.* Charleston, S.C.: Arcadia Publishing, 2000.

McEwen, Tom. *The Gators: A Story of Florida Football.* Huntsville, Ala.: The Strode Publishers, 1974.

Miller, Jeff. *Sunshine Shootouts.* Marietta, Ga.: Longstreet Press, 1992.

Nash, Noel, ed. *The Gainesville Sun Presents Greatest Moments in Florida Gators Football.* Champaign, Ill.: Sports Publishing Inc., 1998.

Smith, Derek. *Glory Yards.* Nashville, Tenn.: Rutledge Hill Press, 1993.

Snook, Jeff. *Year of the Gator.* Nashville, Tenn.: Rutledge Hill Press, 1994.

Spurrier, Steve with Norm Carlson. *Gators: The Inside Story of Florida's First SEC Title.* Orlando, Fla.: Tribune Publishing, 1992.

Stirt, David and Glenn Danforth. *Florida Saturdays at The Swamp: An Inside Look at the Pageantry, Tradition and Spirit of Game Day at the University of Florida.* Champaign, Ill.: Sports Publishing L.L.C., 2004.

Sugar, Bert Randolph. *The SEC.* Indianapolis, Ind.: The Bobbs-Merrill Co., Inc., 1979.

The Gainesville Sun. *Gator Glory: A Season Divine.* Birmingham, Ala.: Sweetwater Press, 1997.

Wuerffel, Danny with Mike Bianchi. *Danny Wuerffel's Tales from the Gator Swamp: Reflections of Faith and Football.* Champaign, Ill.: Sports Publishing L.L.C., 2004.

WEB SITES

2006 Gator Football Media Guide. http://www.gatorzone.com/football/media/#section_g.

Alpha Eta Chapter History. http://grove.ufl.edu/~alphaeta/identity%20files/Alpha%20Eta%20Chapter%20History.pdf

Associated Press. "Florida forces five TOs en route to crucial win over Georgia." http://sports.espn.go.com/ncf/recap?gameId=263010057&confId=null, Oct. 28, 2006.

Associated Press. "Florida QB Leak believes he played with a concussion." http://sports.espn.go.com/ncf/news/story?id=2642824, Oct. 29, 2006.

Associated Press. "Leak accounts for 3 TDs as Florida holds off game Vandy." http://sports.espn.go.com/ncf/recap?gameId=263080238&confId=null, Nov. 4, 2006.

Associated Press. "Two blocked FGs the difference as Florida holds off S. Carolina." http://sports.espn.go.com/ncf/recap?gameId=263150057&confId=null, Nov. 11, 2006.

Associated Press. "No. 3 Florida overwhelms I-AA West Carolina 62–0." http://sports.espn.go.com/ncf/recap?gameId=263220057&confId=null, Nov. 18, 2006.

Associated Press. "Gators win right to face Buckeyes in BCS title game." http://sports.espn.go.com/ncf/news/story?id=2685119, Dec. 3, 2006.

Associated Press. "Florida first to hold football, hoops titles at same time." http://sports.espn.go.com/ncf/bowls06/news/story?id=2724897, Jan. 9, 2007.

Associated Press. "Gators attack: Florida gets title with rout of Ohio

State." http://sports-att.espn.go.com/ncf/recap?gameId=270080194, Jan. 9, 2007.

Associated Press. "Gators, fans celebrate second national championship." http://sports.espn.go.com/ncf/bowls06/news/story?id=2730619, Jan. 13, 2007.

Beard, Franz. "Carlos Alvarez: Meyer Is The Right Coach." Fightin Gators.com. http://florida.scout.com/2/508507.html, March 14, 2006.

Bianchi, Mike. "State of survival: Forget the BCS; Gator fans can be very proud." OrlandoSentinel.com. http://www.orlandosentinel.com/sports/college/gators/orl-bianchi26a06nov26,0,5594966.column?coll=orl-sports-headlines-gators, Nov. 26, 2006.

Bianchi, Mike. "Gators stand alone on top of the sports world." OrlandoSentinel.com. http://www.orlandosentinel.com/sports/college/gators/championship/orl-bianchimetro0907jan09,0,6384838.column, Jan. 9, 2007.

Curtis, Dave. "For Gators, it's win-win: UF clinches berth with help." OrlandoSentinel.com. http://www.orlandosentinel.com/sports/college/gators/orl-uf0506nov05,0,6451490.story?coll=orl-sports-headlines-gators, Nov. 5, 2006.

Dooley, Pat. "Spurrier can't hide glee." Gainesville.com. http://gainesville.com/apps/pbcs.dll/article?AID=/20070404/GATORS02/704040371&SearchID=73277378737522, April 4, 2007.

Gonzalez, Antonio. "Tebow delivers clutch runs, TD: The freshman QB rushes for a critical first down, then scores the winning touchdown." Special to the *Orlando Sentinel.* http://www.orlandosentinel.com/sports/college/gators/orl-ufside1206nov12,0,5130524.story?coll=orl-sports-headlines-gators, Nov. 12, 2006.

Curtis, Dave. "UF ruins Spurrier's return to Swamp: Towering Moss blocks 2 late kicks to preserve victory for the Gators." OrlandoSentinel.com. http://www.orlandosentinel.com/sports/college/gators/orl-uf1206nov12,0,5402910.story?coll=orl-sports-headlines-gators, Nov. 12, 2006.

Curtis, Dave. "Florida 21, Florida State 14: UF makes it 3 in a row against FSU" OrlandoSentinel.com. http://www.orlandosentinel.com/sports/college/gators/orl-uf2606nov26,0,483119.story?coll=orl-sports-headlines-gators, Nov. 26, 2006.

Curtis, Dave. "Saving grace—Tim Tebow got the yards. The Gators kept going." OrlandoSentinel.com. http://www.orlandosentinel.com/sports/college/gators/championship/orl-ufcomebacks0707jan07,0,1661640.story?page=1&coll=orl-home-utility-sports, Jan. 7, 2007.

Curtis, Dave. "Domination in the desert." OrlandoSentinel.com. http://www.orlandosentinel.com/sports/college/gators/championship/orl-bcs0907jan09,0,7048330.story?coll=orl-home-utility-sports, Jan. 9, 2007.

Donnan, Jim. "Florida vs. Ohio State: ESPN's Take." ESPN.com. http://sports.espn.go.com/ncf/bowls06/bowls?game=bcs, Jan. 8, 2007.

ESPN.com news services. "Harvin helps Gators to first SEC title since 2000; BCS title game next?" http://sports.espn.go.com/ncf/recap?gameId=263360057&confId=null, Dec. 2, 2006.

Forde, Pat. "Unconventional attack focuses on creating mismatches." ESPN.com. http://sports.espn.go.com/espn/columns/story?columnist=forde_pat&id=2723273, Jan. 8, 2007.

Forde, Pat. "Florida employs the perfect form against Ohio State." ESPN.com. http://sports.espn.go.com/espn/columns/story?columnist=forde_pat&id=2725029, Jan. 9, 2007.

gatorzone.com. "No. 4 Football Claims Seventh SEC Title With 38-28 Win Over No. 8 Arkansas." http://www.gatorzone.com/story.php?sport=footb&id=11331&html=football/news/20061202111700.html, Dec. 2, 2006.

Gonzalez, Antonio. "Harvey is the ideal defender: Florida defensive end Derrick Harvey rose to the top of his game on college's biggest stage." OrlandoSentinel.com. http://www.orlandosentinel.com/sports/college/gators/championship/orl-ufside0907jan09,0,3779599.story, Jan. 9, 2007.

Hill, Jcmclc. "Southern discomfort in Florida." Page 2, ESPN.com. http://sports.espn.go.com/espn/page2/story?page=hill/070111&lpos=spotlight&lid=tab3pos2, Jan. 11, 2007.

Hobbs, Erika. "Simply fantastic: Florida fans from Gainesville to Glendale, Ariz., to Orlando revel in their team's BCS Championship victory." OrlandoSentinel.com. http://www.orlandosentinel.com/sports/college/gators/championship/orl-fans0907jan09,0,4126815.story, Jan. 9. 2007.

Long, Mark. "Urban Renewal: Meyer Revives Gators." Associated Press. http://hosted.ap.org/dynamic/stories/F/FBC_T25_FLORIDA_RULES?SITE=GAGAI&SECTION=HOME&TEMPLATE=DEFAULT, Jan. 9, 2007.

Schlabach, Mark. "Upstart Arkansas, comeback Gators face off." ESPN.com. http://sports.espn.go.com/ncf/columns/story?columnist=schlabach_mark&id=2682373, Dec. 1, 2006.

Schlabach, Mark. "Tebow's growth as a passer key for Gators." ESPN.com. http://sports.espn.go.com/ncf/columns/story?columnist=schlabach_mark&id=2765329, Feb. 14, 2007.

Whitley, David. "Champs! UF swamps OSU to win national title." OrlandoSentinel.com http://www.orlandosentinel.com/sports/college/gators/championship/orl-mgator1007jan09,0,2468881.story?coll=orl-home-utility-sports, Jan. 9, 2007.

Whitley, David. "How much do you Gators love Mr. Leak now." OrlandoSentinel.com. http://www.orlandosentinel.com/sports/college/gators/championship/orl-whitley0907jan09,0,618862.column?coll=orl-home-utility-sports, Jan. 9, 2007.

INDEX